To Enid and My

On The
Hoof

theology in transit

_- with respect from
Inderjit Bhogal
Sketty
125th Anniversary
9.12.2001_

Inderjit S Bhogal

Penistone Publications

First published in Great Britain in 2001 by Penistone Publications

ISBN: 0-9538793-2-1

Printed in Great Britain by
John Brailsford Print
Rotherham, South Yorkshire

Published by:
Penistone Publications
61 Talbot Road, Penistone,
Sheffield, South Yorkshire, S36 9ED

Introduction

This is a chronicle of theological reflection compiled as Inderjit Bhogal travelled as President of the Methodist Conference during 2000-2001. It offers "theology on the hoof", every bit emerging from an intense, if brief, engagement in many different contexts. The discipline did not allow time for long periods of distillation, reflection and polished pieces of writing, but together these articles contain vividness, freshness and sharpness.

The writings are a practical example of the Urban Theology Unit's vision - that there is an inseparable relationship between personal experience, location, learning and theology. They raise many questions and readers can use them individually or with groups for exploration and discussion. The title 'On The Hoof: theology in transit' encapsulates a belief that our understanding of theology must be developed and explored in the context of today, the people with whom we interact and the places in which we live, work and worship.

Earlier versions of the majority of these reflections were first printed as a fortnightly column in the *Methodist Recorder*; of the others - one appeared in the magazine of the Methodist Church Music Society and the other in *The Methodist Newsletter* in Northern Ireland.

June 2001

Contents

To Meet The People

"It is the duty of a leader to meet the people." These words of Harold Wilson are printed below his statue outside Huddersfield Town Railway Station. I read them several times during Conference week in Huddersfield.

As President of Conference I shall give much time to meeting with people, Methodists and others. I particularly want to meet people who are hurting, or who feel disadvantaged or on the periphery.

On Monday afternoon, 3rd July, at 3.00pm, I met Mrs Doreen Lawrence, Stephen's mother, at the spot where Stephen fell and died. Thirty others from local Methodist Churches were there, including the Rev Harvey Richardson, Chair of the London South East District and Mr Naboth Muchopa, Racial Justice Secretary. We all joined in a vigil with prayer, silence, reading of Scripture, Hymn singing and the lighting of a candle I had taken from Conference. Stephen's father, Neville, had sent apologies because he was out of the country at the time.

I went to that particular spot as President of Conference to honour Stephen, bearing in mind his Methodist heritage. I went also to honour Stephen's Mother and Father for their relentless pursuit of justice and truth. Their commitment is an outstanding contemporary example of Methodist emphasis on social and political holiness.

Doreen Lawrence's visit to Conference in Huddersfield was memorable. It was a privilege for me to welcome her, invite her to address Conference, and then to invite her to sit in Wesley's Chair during the presentation of the Racial Justice business. Speaking to Conference, Mrs Lawrence said it was "time for change" in the nations and the churches.

Stephen, and his family, have already put the nations of England, Wales, Scotland and Ireland, the Churches, the Police and other institutions on the pathways to change. The nations and institutions are challenged to forge new patterns which reject racism and respect all residents and employees, which reject separatism and so enhance the quality of life for us all. In so doing, we will never be able to interpret the life of our nations or churches without reference to the redemptive and transforming suffering of Stephen, Doreen and Neville Lawrence.
Doreen welcomed me when I arrived for the vigil. She then showed me the marks

7

on the Plaque dedicated to the memory of Stephen. Racist vandals have again attempted to damage the Memorial.

Stephen is a martyr of our age. Whatever else is taken away from us, no-one can take our martyrs from us. Nations and churches are given new light and life by martyrs. The spot that marks Stephen's murder is sacred. If people deface or attempt to destroy the Plaque here, it is because they realise that Stephen and his memory lives on to influence change so that people give life to each other, not kill each other. They will never erase our memory of Stephen.

My next official engagement was a visit to the Isles of Scilly which meant that I met people in one of the remotest Circuits in the Connexion.

To reach parts of the Circuit, I travelled by land, air and sea. I had been invited to share in the Centenary celebrations at St Mary's. I was only the third President of Conference to visit these very beautiful Isles.

St Mary's Chapel was decorated with imaginative floral creations depicting local life. Their perfume made me realise why these Isles are also called the Isles of Scent. After morning worship commencing at 11.00am, I was to accompany the Minister, Rev Brian Mavers, to conduct worship at St Martin's Chapel. We were to depart on a boat at 2.00pm. Brian said, "It's either a short sermon or a quick lunch!" A quick lunch then, I thought!

After preaching here in September 1743, John Wesley wrote in his Journal, "It was a blessed time, so that I scarce knew how to conclude."

Len Michell, Local Preacher, organist and local historian, had written a history of St Mary's for the Centenary. I asked him how many black or Asian people had preached at St Mary's. "Not one," he said, "You are the first one." Mr Michell's publication is most illuminating. It speaks of "exciting....exhausting....and testing times" in St Mary's. When the Chapel was opened the Minister, Rev Wescott, had written: "Large crowds of people gathered (people of all the islands were represented)...sectarian bigotry, if any had previously existed, was for the time forgotten. People (of different denominations) met together as though they were all members of one community." The same could be said about the Centenary celebrations.

The Chapel was practically full for the Centenary celebrations. In addition to the Islanders, in attendance were "incomers" and holiday makers. The congregation included Presbyters who had ministered in the Circuit previously; Rev Ward Davies, Rev Ronald Crewes and Rev Ian Haile, the former Chair of Cornwall District. Mr Haile also confessed that he was a member of the District Committee in Wolverhampton and Shrewsbury which had recommended me as a Candidate for ministry.

The boat "Surprise" took Brian Mavers and me over very choppy waters to St Martin's. Twelve members gathered at the Chapel and provided a lavish tea. Later, holiday makers swelled the numbers at worship. I learned a new word, "incomers", a reference to anyone who migrates to the Isles of Scilly. Incomers now outnumber the born and bred Islanders. I preached in St Martin's on the theme of "Islanders and Incomers." St Martin's Chapel has one of the finest views I have seen. It is quite a contrast to the view of brokenness from Wincobank Chapel on the flower estate in Sheffield where I am based. I sat on a rock outside the Chapel and drank in the nectar of fresh air and outstanding scenery.

The following day "Kingfisher II" took me across a slightly calmer sea to Tresco. I wanted to visit the three Methodist members on this exotic small island. They said to me that the only Christian expression possible on the Island is ecumenical, though they miss Methodist worship. The Dorrien-Smith family has run Tresco as a private estate since the 1830's. They have developed the Abbey Gardens and filled them with rare plants. The fauna and flora in the Gardens, so much of it African, took me back to Kenya.

Hilary Tabron met me off the boat and gave me a guided tour of the island, including of course a visit to the Gardens where we had coffee with Lorraine, who is a member of staff there. We ended up at the Primary School where Derek Tabron is Head Teacher. The School has 21 pupils. When I asked the children what it is like on the island, the first thing they said was that they felt "safe".

So, do our children and young people have to live in places like Tresco to be safe? What do we need to do to be in connexion with young people, black and white, and enable them to be safe wherever they are? What needs to be done to ensure that we are constantly in connexion with the remotest Circuits?

As I took a last look at the scenery outside St Martin's Chapel, blue sea and white sands, one islander came and stood by me and said, "That's Harold Wilson's favourite view."

3rd August 2000

Strength From The Hills

19,000 children die each day because of poverty. At the same time, the age of 100 is not uncommon today. One of my neighbours who died this year was exactly 100 years older than Anjuli, who was 9 in January.

One person I hoped might live to 100 (January 2001) was Bert Bissell. He died at the age of 96. On 7th August, 2000 I visited his grave in the cemetery in Glen Nevis at the foot of his beloved Ben Nevis. I stood beside it with members of the Vicar Street Bible Class, and friends from Lochaber, for a short vigil of remembrance. The Revd. Alan Davies, one of 20 members of the Class who have been ordained into Presbyteral Ministry in different denominations, led us in Prayers, Reading of Scripture, Reflections and Silence. I prayed with open eyes. There was a stillness, a slight drizzle, and a scent of Pine in the air. It was clear to me, as someone had commented, that "if there is a reconstitution, resuscitation and resurrection of the body one day, Bert's first sight will be Ben Nevis." Heaven.

I first met Bert Bissell in September 1964, just a few days after I had moved with my family to Dudley in the Midlands. We had moved into rented accommodation in New Road with the Sandher family, from which Jasbir took me to Vicar Street Methodist Church. Jasbir and a dozen or so other young Asian men were already attending the "Fireside" Meeting there on Monday evenings. They were there because Bert Bissell had naturally visited them when they had moved into Dudley, or greeted them in the street and befriended them. The "Fireside" became an important weekly gathering point for a number of us. We formed a football team, the Panjab Rovers, and ran it from the "Fireside" - and won a few trophies. I was goalkeeper. Bert Bissell used to come and cheer us on at our matches.

Bert Bissell was an "old man" all the time I knew him. Yet he had a youthful approach to life, and always had the capacity to relate to younger people. He led the Young Men's Bible Class for almost 80 years, influencing scores of people. It is often asked why so few men go to Church. The male leaders in Churches have some explaining to do. Bert Bissell did at least try to address this issue, and tried to help men to find meaning, purpose and faith in life.

The Young Men's Bible Class has always been well attended. The Class has always met at 3.00pm on a Sunday afternoon, a time that in recent years has clashed with live football on TV. A Liturgy of four hearty hymns, Bible Reading, and an Address, is hardly an exciting prospect. So what attracted men to the Class meetings? Members have often remarked that Bert Bissell trusted and respected each individual. He had the ability to give time, attention and a listening ear to each person. This was simply his lifestyle. His inspiration and model, he would say, was "the young man of Nazareth, Jesus Christ." More than this, he helped people to relate faith to daily life, and find excitement in sport and mountain climbing. As a life long supporter of Coventry City Football Club and Worcestershire Cricket Club, he organised regular Match outings. One of his favourite walks was a night climb up Snowdon and, of course, his climbs up Ben Nevis. The mountain climbing appealed very much to me.

I joined Class members on several night climbs up Snowdon and have continued the practice. Occasionally, it is a privilege to experience the sun rise from the summit. I joined Bert Bissell's groups also on visits to Fort William and to climb Ben Nevis. I went for 12 consecutive years from 1965, including interrupting placements as a Student Minister in order to do this. One year, I privately arranged a placement with Duncansburgh Parish Church, Fort William, to spend some extra time in the area and to walk in the Glen Nevis area. In 1968, I was part of a group that helped to carry a Tablet of stone, sent from Hiroshima, to the summit of Ben Nevis. It weighed one hundredweight. We were assisted by a team of young people from Sheffield who were camping in Glen Nevis.

All the memories and thoughts, and many others, were part of conversations when I returned to Fort William this month. This time I went with my family - Kathy, Liamarjit and Anjuli. On the way, we met up with the Revd Sue Jansen, who trained for ministry at UTU and has served in Glasgow. It was good to be in Fort William, and to be there as President of Conference. We stayed with the Revd Alan and Mrs Margaret Davies. He was once the assistant to President of Conference and the Records Secretary of Conference. He was instrumental in the creation of the designation "RR" (Recognised and Regarded as Methodist Minister), and is a former Chair of the Lincoln and Grimsby District. For 14 years Alan worked with the Home Mission Division and had responsibility for the Luton Industrial College and Church in Rural Life. Conference gave Alan "permission to sit down" seven years ago. He has since then made a positive contribution to the life of Churches in the Western Highlands, especially Church of Scotland parishes. Alan has always been an encouragement to me. I was glad to visit him and affirm his continuing ministry. I preached in Duncansburgh (Fort William) and Duror Parish Churches on the 6th August, Hiroshima Day and Transfiguration Day.

The following day, after the vigil at Bert Bissell's graveside, I led a Pilgrimage up Ben Nevis. The party included the four Bhogals, Mr Astley Blake who succeeded Bert Bissell as President of the Bible Class, Daljit Sandher, who also played with Panjab Rovers, Mr Barry Weetman from the Methodist Recorder and his son, Matthew. John Tranter from Whittington Moor Methodist Church, Chesterfield, had found out about this Pilgrimage and made his own way to join us. We were led by two experienced local climbers, Mr Duncan Haggart (aged 70) and Mr Keith Hamilton (aged 68). We reached the summit in four hours, the fastest time in my experience! Anjuli reached the summit first.

On the summit I was introduced to Mr Brian McDermott of the local Mountain Rescue Team. He had spent three nights and four days up there to repair the Peace Cairn, first built by Bert Bissell and a group that included Alan Davies in 1945 to celebrate the end of the War and as a symbol of prayers for peace. I've never seen the cairn so secure. It has been moved a little so that it is closer to the ruins of a weather observatory (built in 1880) and the Trig Point. "This is where people gather," said Brian, "they are more likely to see it here and to get it's message. It may also help to draw more respect for Ben Nevis and the summit from the climbers." Brian said that the John Muir Trust, owners of Ben Nevis, respect the peace cairn. I also hope that the new owners will keep access to Ben Nevis available and free to climbers. Brian comes from 'Derry in Northern Ireland. He explained his work to repair the peace cairn to weary, cold pilgrims as snowy rain soaked us. I led a short act of remembrance and prayer. The rain fell on us all the way down.

We reached base at 5.00pm. After showers and a warm meal, the Bhogals were heading home on board the Scotrail Caledonian Sleeper. In the early hours of the following morning (8th August), Liamarjit was 11 years old. I wonder if the age of 100 will be even more common in 89 years time, and if children will no longer die because of poverty.

17th August 2000

Challenging Black Christians

"Pride and Prejudice" is a publication edited by Mr Naboth Muchopa, Connexional Secretary for Racial Justice. It was recently published and contains stories which illustrate the very positive contribution black Methodists are making in Church and Society. There are, of course, many whose story has to be discovered through personal meeting and listening. For example, there is Deacon Harriet Bacon who came from Barbados three years ago. I met her in Weston-Super-Mare while I was there for World Village. Harriet is living and working in Locking Castle, a new Housing Estate. She has built up a worshipping community that has increased from ten to fifty during her time. Such encounters have inspired me this summer as I have attended a number of important Conferences.

Phyllis Thompson of the New Testament Church of God was one of the staff on the Zebra Project in London. Phyllis and I were Youth Representatives in the British Team to attend a World Council of Churches meeting in Melbourne, Australia in 1980. She now works in education. We were both speakers at a ground breaking national conference of Britain's Black Majority Churches (BMCs) held in Brighton.

The multiplication and growth of BMCs has been a significant development in Britain over the last fifty years. Christian witness and worship in many city centres and inner city areas would be seriously weakened if the BMCs were not there. Local ecumenism has yet to embrace this factor though there is a greater awareness of it today. Bishop Joel Aldred, Director of the Birmingham based Centre for Black and White Christian Partnership, has also stated that there has been "a dearth of co-operation between BMCs" because of the sheer scale of their growth. Mr Mark Sturge, General Secretary of the African Caribbean Evangelical Alliance, organiser of the Conference, feels the time has come for BMCs to come together and to "play a wider role in this country's national life." Some 500 people attended the Conference. The organisers had expected 5,000. I led a Seminar on "Challenges facing Churches today" and addressed the main Conference, reminding participants that there were significant numbers of black Christians making important contributions in "white majority Churches."

There are two million Asians of various national origins living in Britain. Approximately 50,000 of them are Christians. Many of them come to Britain as Refugees or Asylum Seekers. Most of them worship in Asian majority congregations. Pradip Sudra, Secretary of the Alliance of Asian Christians, has done much to bring Asian Christians together. Naturally, he was prime mover behind a Conference on "British Asian Discipleship" that was held at Cliff College, Derbyshire. The dates for this Conference sadly clashed with the BMC event. I managed to juggle with dates and transport to put in an appearance at both.

Three hundred and fifty attended the Asian Christians Conference. Many white Christians representing organisations with a "mission among Asians" were there. In my Address, I briefly shared my own journey of faith and said what I find compelling in the story of Jesus. I also quoted Sadhu Sundar Singh who said that the Gospel is best communicated with Indians using Indian modes of thought. He drew a contrast between the English "china" tea cup, and the Indian clay bowl to illustrate his point. Different cultural norms have to be respected. One of the questions addressed in this Conference was: "What does Christian theology look like from an Asian perspective?" Listen to what Asian people have to say in answer.

There are significant numbers of Asian Christians making their mark in white majority churches also. The numbers of Asian Christians are growing too. Many are discovering new meaning and faith and patterns of discipleship in the story of Jesus Christ. I would add to the words of Bishop Aldred that black and Asian Christians need to forge greater co-operation too. This needs to happen alongside developments of partnership between black, Asian and white Christians.

I attended the Black Methodists' Group (BMG) Conference on the theme of "Black Health in the New Millennium." The BMG has its origins in the Black Methodist Ministers' Group formed in 1985 "to provide support and fellowship for a small number of Black Methodist Ministers in the British Conference by creating opportunities for sharing experiences, discussion and social interaction." I was a founding members of the Group, and am a former Treasurer and Chair of the Group. The Methodist Conference has supported the Group's existence (Faithful and Equal Report 1987). BMG has an established meeting at the annual Methodist Conference, and an established programme. There are Methodists who say that the existence of the BMG is "separatist." I do not agree. The Group exists and makes a positive contribution alongside all the other various Methodist groups.

I have a concern for everyone's well-being. I have a particular concern for the health of black people. The BMG Conference was made aware by Prof. Fred

Hickling that "migration dislocates and dismembers people." Most migration is from rural agricultural contexts to urban contexts. This has a huge detrimental effect on health. A Government report highlights that black and Asian people are prone to hypertension, diabetes and strokes. I was reminded that the life expectancy of Asian men in the UK is fifty five. Better get more mountain air!

Black Methodists are torn in a situation of tension. We want to make a positive contribution in the life of the Church. Because we have yet to achieve significant participation, the few who do get involved are liable to get exhausted and have early burn out. Black Methodists, and the whole Church needs to address this in the interests of the health of us all. The Revd. Dr Emmanuel Lartey (Chair of the BMG) gave the Conference valuable African insights on why, under what circumstances, we survive and thrive. He drew on the theme of relationships with God, oneself, others, with/within Groups, and with spaces/earth. A fracture in any relationship harms well-being. Mending broken relationships heals. The Conference was most worthwhile. Absent members missed a treat. Churches should encourage black Methodists to attend such gatherings.

The Third annual Black Methodists Youth Conference (BMYC) was held at King's Park, Northampton, and attracted an attendance of forty five. The focus was on Leadership. Naboth Muchopa convenes this important gathering. The Methodist Conference this year was made aware that there were no black representatives under the age of 25, and as a matter of "urgency" took action to remedy this for the future. The Church needs black leadership. The BMG and BMYC are of strategic importance in the efforts to develop black leadership. My basic message to the participants of the BMYC was "Be a Leader".

I was glad to attend the BMYC. It gave me opportunity to spend time with potential young black leaders. I listened to their stories of pride and pain. I enjoyed their eloquence and fun, and learned from their insights. It was disturbing though to hear young black Methodists tell of their personal experiences of "stop and search" by the Police, and of harassment by Police. In order to ensure that young people, black and white, can use their experiences and gifts in Church, members need to make contact with and to meet with them. I hope my attendance at the BMYC was affirming and will symbolise my desire to see the Church take positive action to re-member young black Methodists. All credit to Mr Muchopa for convening and facilitating the BMYC. His assistants included Mr Barry Troupe, a Youth Worker in Birmingham, and Sam Wilkins. Sam sings with Soul and Spirit, the Group that sang so inspirationally in the Methodist Conference Service.

Robert Beckford is the Theologian who is pushing out the boundaries of British Black Theology. His books "Jesus is Dread" and "Dread and Pentecostalism" are a significant contribution. In "Dread and Pentecostalism" he particularly challenges black Christians to engage with political issues and public life. He calls for a historical, social and theological analysis and reflection on the experiences of black people in Britain. Black people have to analyse, reflect on and interpret their own experiences. No-one else can do this correctly.

31st August 2000

Seeds of Hope in Kenya

Dust. Red - powder thin soil. In parts, Kenya is a dust bowl. Since the El Niño torrents in 1997 it has not rained, the severest drought in the country for thirty years. Kathy, Liamarjit, Anjuli and I spent a fortnight in Kenya during August. Every day it was cloudy. There was the early morning dew, but, tantalisingly, no rain.

Having lived on coffee farms in my younger days, I was distressed to see feeble, withering coffee plants. Eighty per cent of Kenya's labour force is employed in agriculture. Coffee and tea are the nation's principal exports. Please keep purchasing these, preferably through Traidcraft and Fair Trade.

With a dwindling agricultural base, there is a steady migration of people from the "interior" countryside to the cities. Maasai herders, in their bright red garments, normally reluctant to rub shoulders with "Gentiles", now face the ultimate dilemma of pasturing their African humped cattle along the Uhuru Highway in the centre of Nairobi. We saw them in suburbs like Lavington, and even outside the gates of President Moi's State Home.

This is, of course, an additional threat to the "Shambas" (Gardens) of people who, out of need, are planting vegetables alongside Nairobi's highways. Some people are eking out a livelihood on the only bit of land available to them. There are cabbages, onions, carrots being carefully nurtured. Water is purchased at increasing cost for them. I chatted with Jackson who, having given a little water to his cabbages, was covering the root area with dry grass. "To prevent evaporation," he said. Jackson is a Security Guard at a Restaurant in Lavington. He grows his vegetables outside the Restaurant's gates. His food is threatened by lead from vehicle exhaust fumes, lack of water, passers by and now cattle too.

The roads, cut up by El Niño floods, have not been repaired. Carrying Juggernauts they were never built for, there are now pot holes like craters in places. Kenya is ranked one of the worst places for road accidents in the world. Children resorting to begging in streets are exposed to another danger. We saw those who had been hit by cars. One man had died, his blood forming a pool on the parched earth.

The drought is biting hard. It is affecting every person, plant and animal. Kenya's economy is on a downward spiral, increasing the levels of corruption and crime.

Having visited Kenya four years ago and experienced a buoyant nation, it was alarming to see a Kenya so hard hit by the drought. We read of floods in India, forest fires in USA, water on the North Pole. Weather systems, affected by human lifestyles, now threaten human life. It is common wisdom in Kenya that "the drought is the result of deforestation in the country. We have sold our birth right with our trees. All we have now is God."

In the midst of this, the abiding images that will remain for me, out of this visit, are of welcome, hospitality and hope in the midst of scarce resources. At Kianjai Church, near Meru in the north, a District Women's Meeting burst into song and dance to welcome the Bhogals. "When a visitor returns home they are welcome" they sang in the Kimeru dialect. Then a table, with a meal of vegetable and banana mix and stew. At Ribe, near Mombasa, within sight of the spot where the Methodist Church in Kenya was born in 1862, a table was set. We were fed with tea made with local milk (no water), and doughnuts. Delicious. Just below us was a Shamba where members have planted forty banana trees, twelve orange trees, thirty mango trees and ten coconut trees. No rain, but people keep planting in hope. People welcomed us and fed us in their homes, even when electricity was cut off and all was dark. We were treated as guests of honour and in each context I felt as if I was on the Mount of Transfiguration. Like Peter, I found myself saying, "It is good to be here. I wish I could stay here."

With more people moving into built up areas, the Church will need to give greater attention to urban mission and ministry. The earlier initiatives have concentrated on the provision of education. There are numerous superb School projects, and the Kenya Methodist University (KEMU), now three years old, is reflecting maturity in quality. Urban housing, health and transport pose urgent needs that affect the quality of life. These three issues come together, for example, in the lives of children dodging trucks and buses in the streets. Twelve months ago in Meru, the Methodist Church began the Kaaga Street Children's Project. They are in contact with ninety seven children who live and sleep along the streets. Currently twelve of them are in the Project's home and school. "Our impact is meagre owing to lack of funds," says the Kaaga Synod Bishop, Rev Wilfred Kaburu. "We hope to take in eight more children soon. We are serving a mid-day meal three times a week in the streets. The demand is greater than the resources we have, but we have a lot of love to share."

At Kiandegwa, near Nairobi, is a tiny wooden structure which is the local Methodist Chapel. Next to it is a small Health Clinic. The buildings are surrounded by paddy fields growing rice. They are watered by bore holes and so green in comparison to the red soil. We reached the area by car, leaving a dense fog of dust in our tracks. Here we found people being assisted with relief food supplies. Locally grown rice is exported. To feed others, the people in the area work in disease infected fields. The stagnant water attracts mosquitoes. The Methodist Clinic treats people for Malaria and other water born diseases, and iron deficiency. In the Chapel, 14 kilos of maize per family were being distributed. Such relief work is involving Ecumenical co-operation between the Methodist Church in Kenya, the Full Gospel Church, the Independent Pentecostal Church, the Roman Catholic Church and the Anglican Church in Kenya.

There is also the Methodist Hospital based in Maua. We were welcomed there by Dr Claire Smithson, Sister Barbara Dickinson and Paul, Rachel and Hannah Lindoewood. They have served in Maua for between six and twenty years. I asked them if Maua is a place people get hooked or trapped by. "It's a bit of both!" they said. In the main, they enjoy life in Maua in spite of some "recent struggles" which included, on the days we visited, running the hospital without water. Here too, the largest cause of sickness is malaria.

A most memorable visit was to Landhia Mawe ("stone houses"). This is a small housing estate by the Railway Station. At the heart of it is a small Ramgharia Railways Sikh Temple. This was the estate on which I lived for the first eleven years of my life.

The presence of Asians in East Africa goes back well over three thousand years. They were used by the Portuguese to build Fort Jesus in Mombasa four hundred years ago. From 1895 Asian labourers were used by the British to build a 600 mile railway line from Mombasa to Kisumu. The builders reached "Nyrobi" (a Maasai word meaning "place of cool, fresh waters") in 1898 and rested here before tackling the Great Rift Valley. Many of the labourers were Sikhs. They built a small Temple right by the line. My own family came into Kenya with the "indentured" labour brought in from India. There is a photograph of my Grandfather and Father, along with others who helped make modern Nairobi, in the Nairobi Museum. It was good to share this part of our history with the children.

We visited the Temple. We visited the house I and my family lived in. The backyard of the house is now used to make beds for Refugees! Maasai were pasturing cattle by the house. The Temple is sadly about to be closed as a result of persistent vandalism.

Modern Nairobi is 100 years old this Millennium year. It was a significant year in which to go and touch my roots. It was important to travel with Kathy, Liamarjit and Anjuli so that they could see part of our heritage. We visited my old school, the Sikh Khalsa Boys and Girls School, too. It was an inspiration to catch a vision of the Methodist Church in Kenya sowing seeds of hope in a tough environment.

As we prepared to catch the return flight, I noticed my shoes were covered in dust. I could not bring myself to shake off this dust. We had been so well received. It was good to walk in the soil on which I took birth.

May God bless Kenya with rain in the coming rain season, cool, refreshing, life-giving rain.

14th September 2000

Tables, Triangles and Tea Towel

"The preacher this morning is brother of Hardial Bhogal, Chief Executive of Walsall Council," boasted Leslie Griffiths, minister at Wesley's Chapel. He had met my brother the previous day (2.9.00) at the opening of the new premises at Walsall Central Hall where Hardial had read a lesson and "sung all the Hymns".

I mounted Wesley's Pulpit ignoring the "no entry" sign by the steps, for the first time. It was good to preach from this pulpit as occupant of Wesley's chair. Later, I celebrated Holy Communion at "Wesley's Table". What a delight it was to eat at this Table with people of all ages, of different national backgrounds with so many of them in their national costumes. Among them – Princess Angelica of Tonga and the Vice President. My eyes moved between the congregation before me, and the stained glass window above them in the gallery showing John Wesley the preacher surrounded by people of different nations. "The world is my Parish". The world is in Wesley's Chapel and John Wesley would be delighted too.

After this celebration a lavish meal with many around a table that practically filled a large room in Wesley's manse.

I was thus inducted into the new Methodist Connexional Year. September comes and the Methodist Church seems to engage into second gear having taken the foot off the accelerator for the summer. Of course, pressures do not ease off completely in August. Unresolved issues demand attention.

The Vice President and I commenced our round of District visits. We began in the Wolverhampton and Shrewsbury District with a joint ten day visit. We chose to begin here not only because of my special associations with the District but also because it is a District that embraces Wales. We stood on Wenlock Edge and Long Mynd in the lovely county of Shropshire and looked over to the Welsh Peaks that beckoned us and saluted the Vice President.

What a variety of tables I sat at, and ate at. There were the tables in Town Halls for Civic Receptions in three "Black Country" metropolitan Boroughs of Dudley, Walsall and Wolverhampton. In Dudley Town Hall, overlooking the castle and coronation gardens, members of my family joined us. In Walsall it was a great delight to sit with Hardial at the superb round teak table in his office from which he manages sixty members of staff and an annual budget of £300m. In Wolverhampton the Ravi Dassi Sikh mayor Mr Tarseim Singh and the Chief

Executive Mr Darren Anderson of Christian faith and Afro-Carribbean roots hosted a reception. In attendance – members of Low Hill, Fordhouses, Stratton St. and Darlington St. Methodist churches and Wolverhampton Inter-Faith Group that I served with, and members of the Council.

I was privileged to be welcomed by and to eat with people of different cultures and faiths. How would Enoch Powell respond to these developments?

We sat in Telford Town Hall with the Chief Executive and colleagues in their Board Room discussing what regeneration, anti-poverty and anti-racism strategies mean in a New Town (now nearly 40 years old). We sat at the table driving the development of the Brierly Hill Triangle building on the "success" of Merry Hill shopping centre discussing "what is the spirituality of this centre?" We sat around a table in a farmhouse kitchen to hear of poverty, stress and suicide in farming communities. We met and talked with inmates and chaplains in a Young Offenders Remand Centre (Brinsford, Featherstone) and heard of conditions that can promote or prevent suicide among the inmates.

The questions that are raised for me in such contexts are – who sits at the tables where decisions are made and power is exercised? Who else should be there? And what is the role of the church at these tables? How do we ensure that people who sit around tables in decision making reflect the communities whose lives are affected by the decisions made?

In Brinsford the Methodist chaplain, the Revd Alan Francom, showed me and the Revd Peter Curry (chair: Wolverhampton and Shrewsbury district) around. It was clear how much his friendship and support is valued. Within the atmosphere of iron railings, reinforced doors, locks, chains and keys there is room for up to 500 young people awaiting sentence. We met young people full of hopes. Young black people appeared to be the majority present. The chaplains and governor later told us at the lunch table that "black youngsters make up about thirty percent of those in the centre, the national average." One thing that was confirmed for me is that if churches want to make contact with young black people we will only meet many of them in remand centres and prisons. But why are their numbers here disproportionate to the percentage of Black people (six percent) in the British population? No evidence here that police are being lenient with black people.

The "inmates" of all shades of skin colour were glad to see me too, and readily told me about themselves. In one room a Maths class was taking place. They were focussing on triangles. "A bit like the Trinity isn't it?" enquired the teacher looking in my direction. "The Trinity is not a triangle", I said, and immediately the Maths class had become a theological discussion. Nonchurchiatric young people – theology – impromptu - in a young offenders centre.

The triangle, like tables, was a recurrent feature in discussions. At Merry Hill shopping centre we were introduced to the "Brierly Hill Triangle". A line drawn between these shops, the Brierly Hill High Street, and waterfront offices forms a triangle. The area within it is being proposed for a new development which will eventually shift the commercial hub of the borough of Dudley to Brierley Hill. What does this do to the surrounding neighbourhoods, traffic in the area, and more particularly to Dudley town centre already affected by Merry Hill?

At the Wolverhampton and Shrewsbury District Synod part of the discussions centred on "Connexional leadership" which is perceived by many in terms of a pyramidal hierarchy. How do we move on from the images of centres and margins and hierarchies to those of level playing fields where we are all part of the team and share in leadership corporately? One thing that must be affirmed again and again is that the local church is connexional, every bit as anyone or any Body we term connexional. The local church is at the heart of the connexion. What I am finding is that this heart is warm, even if aching.

Triangles are lovely shapes, but I can't think about them without thinking Bermuda. Triangles in remand centres? Triangles in development? Triangles in Connexion? Who and what is in danger of disappearing here?

The last words on my visit to the District belong to a friend called Rachel who is disabled. I had not seen Rachel for some years. "I love you," she remarked when we met. She works in the kitchen at Wednesbury Central Hall. While the Vice-President and I shared in an evaluation of our visit, Rachel stood at the kitchen sink and "did the dishes". She washed and dried the dishes. Before departing, I went to see Rachel to say farewell. Tea towel in hand, she wanted to take a closer look at the "Presidential Cross" around my neck. "Is that a dove?" she asked pointing to the central symbol on it. From a distance it looks like a dove. "It shows a water jug, a wash basin and a tea towel. These symbols come from the story of Jesus doing some washing up," I said, "to me it says to be President is to be a servant, and that ministry can be seen in the midst of water jugs and wash basins and tea towels." Rachel immediately said, "I'm a minister!"

28th September 2000

"We will, we will rock you"

"To be treated like you," spoke out the voice of a little Romanian boy sitting bare foot on a mound of rubble. This is his prayer. In his words this includes having "a house with flowers, a bicycle, a dog and a family." His appeal was used on video by World Action, the youth campaign arm of the Methodist Church, at the launch of "Streets Apart" during Breakout 2000 held at London's Docklands Arena. Some twelve million children, from the very young to those approaching adulthood, are driven to live on streets and need protection. There are children who live in appalling conditions throughout the world. The names of the nearby Docks brought to mind the street children of India. But many street children are in Europe and Britain. They live in danger from attack, abuse, rape, hunger, drugs, disease and also from slavery, sex and arms trades, among other menaces.

The Streets Apart Campaign received the support of participants arriving for worship on the Sunday morning at the London Weekend. We removed and deposited a sock each into a plastic bag to express solidarity. Shoes and feet are symbols of power, prowess and status. I removed and gave the pair of socks I was wearing. The socks are to be taken to 10 Downing Street, asking Government to act to protect street children. During prayers, worshippers removed a shoe to stand on the bare foot and pledge their commitment with words of a specially written promise.

As I said them, I recalled playing barefoot in Kenya. It's painful to stub a toe on a rock, or to have a thorn pierce the skin. I have a scar where a large piece of broken glass cut my foot. At least it toughened the skin on my feet, which may contribute to my ability to walk long distances without getting blisters.

There were not many yellow or green socks though, not even among the many hardened MAYC - Breakout punters. In every other respect, we appeared to be Norwich City Football Club Supporters, or is there more street-cred in being Brazil fans, or were we Australians relishing their Olympic success! On the London Underground or the Docklands Light Railway, the chanting of "oggy, oggy, oggy - oi, oi, oi" was accompanied by the Mexican Wave. It was the atmosphere of an FA Cup Final Day. Onlookers appeared curious or bemused and some asked who we were.

It was the annual Methodist Youth Extravaganza. Breakout 2000 provided an opportunity for a young people's rave-up, and for some older people to allow their youthfulness to shine through, and to let our hair down (if we have any). A solidarity in spirit bringing the ages together. It was fun. This year the event was ecumenical and supported by Churches Together in England (CTE). The joint Churches Youth Service of CTE assisted with planning. Anglicans, Baptists, Roman Catholics, Salvation Army and New Testament Church of God were among those who shared with Methodists.

CTE sponsorship did not mean that Scotland, Wales and Ireland were not represented. I met groups from different parts of these nations. An Exchange group from Zimbabwe accompanied their Saltash hosts. Many were from rural contexts where young people can feel isolated. There was a group of sixty, for example, with Rev Ruth and Dr John Parry from Cowling near Skipton. A meter-and-half- long yellow and green Worm, partner Wormetta, and some little Wormlets, accompanied their caring keepers from Bromsgrove. They will all have spent a fair amount of money in order to attend. Sleeping on church hall floors is part of the fun - well, some at least slept.

The two generations of the Bhogal family joined the revellers in Leicester Square for clowning, miming, magic, steel band music, singing and prayer on the busy streets of London. Joel Edwards Jnr led songs by the Empire Cinema. He said this street presentation was about "proclaiming the Gospel, giving some encouragement to young people and showing that we're not all just serious". One performer invited me to help to tie him up with a long metal chain and a padlock. He then wriggled his way out in 35 seconds. "You can be set free from the chains of sin in less time," he said, "all it takes is one prayer."

Just then, a group of young men standing by me got into discussion. Before long we were into the political hot potato of petrol prices. One view was that the prices should be reduced. I suggested that was a selfish line to take, and not very environmentally friendly. Sin came into the discussion again. I said that sin is a little word with "I" in the middle. Sin is selfishness. Sin is about being selfish to the point of being destructive. We can see such destructiveness in human exhaustion, environmental pollution, poverty and debt, the fact of street children. Does the green and yellow version of the Jubilee 2000 chain we were wearing, and all the frustrations of the debt cancellation campaign, suggest that the chains of sin have many knots and take much prayer, sweat, blood and tears, and many years to unravel?

Breakout 2000 demonstrated considerable enthusiasm and energy in the younger members of churches to grapple with issues at depth, some in various workshops. London Arena oozed with life. Ibiza dance tunes, dances, football, netball, songs and other vocal offerings, drama, laughter, clapping, foot stamping, swaying, balloons, pom-poms, live bands including Delirious, and Methodist DJ, the Rev Ralph Ward of Bacup. The London Arena was transformed into a mega youth club.

An inter-active, multi-media, visual feast with light, sound, colour and human heat. "We will, we will rock you" from the Queen Rock Band, alongside choruses like "I found Jesus" and the current favourite "The History Maker." Quite a formula for a contemporary Rock Spirituality. It is a spirituality that reflects a maturity and can move on from the younger rocking of the lullaby "I will rock you, rock you, rock you." I warmed very much to this spirituality but offer questions for exploration. Is there space within the Rock Spirituality of inter-activity, sound and movement, for emptiness, silence and stillness? Can the "I" in "I've found Jesus" move on to a shout of "We will rock you" to the structures of selfish sinful injustice?

The organising team should be congratulated. They felt Breakout 2000 had been a "heart-warming event" though they had expected "more than 5,000 to be here." Most participants found it exciting and worthwhile. The numbers did swell to 8,000 for the Sunday morning worship as local congregations joined in. Thanks and best wishes to Mark Wakelin, the ex-MAYC National Secretary who is now Director of the North Bank Estate's Centre for Christian Living in Muswell Hill. Welcome and best wishes to the new MAYC National Secretary, Mike Seaton. Mike is well aware of the challenges and opportunities that face him and his team as they plan for the future. There is a strong base to build on, and ecumenical support can strengthen Breakout which can be developed as a resource to local Youth Leaders, Youth Groups and Congregations.

Sockless, though not barefoot, I went on the Jubilee Line to the Millennium Dome, another place disappointed with numbers. Having followed the Dome debate though, I was surprised by the numbers in attendance, some 28,000, which is more than they had at West Ham Football Club the day before. There were long queues for most sites, and not a spare seat under the great canopy for the show.

The Jubilee Line in Scripture leads to debt cancellation and redistribution of land. On the way to the Dome, and travelling around the Docklands area generally, attention is drawn to imposing, erect, glass buildings. No more rock and concrete. What do all these buildings reflect? At a time when so much distrust and criticism is directed at contemporary structures, the ones inside can scrutinise the area anonymously.   At the same time, we on the outside gaze at these constructions - we see only ourselves and our communities reflected in them. Dome, Debt, Street Children - it's all part of the reflection of the world we have created.   A striking context in which to discern the God who rocked Egypt and Babylon, and who could cause water to flow in the wilderness of rock.

12th October 2000

Prayer And Politics Go Hand In Hand

"Before you go – I would like my President to say a prayer". This was the request of Mr Paul Boateng MP and Methodist Local Preacher. We were in the middle of a crowded Hotel lounge in Brighton, at the Labour Party Conference, and had just spent an hour or so together. Our conversation had touched on issues related to Prison Inspectors, Prison Chaplaincy, racism in prisons, and the detention of Asylum seekers in conventional prisons. Rachel Lampard, Methodist Secretary for parliamentary and political affairs accompanying me, and Mr Boateng bowed their heads, and I offered a prayer. A memorable symbol of the partnership between prayer and politics. I recalled the words of Jesus, "where two or three are gathered in my name I am there in the midst of them", and felt deeply honoured to be invited to pray.

Over the last month or so I have visited the Party Political Conferences of Liberal Democrats, Labour and Conservatives. In addition I have met with Mr William Hague, leader of the Conservative Party at the Conservative Central Office, and also Mr Tony Blair, Prime Minister, and Mr Jack Straw, Home Secretary, at 10 Downing Street. I hope to meet Mr Charles Kennedy, leader of the Liberal Democrats soon. To my regret, I was not able to accept an invitation to attend the TUC Conference owing to pressure of other commitments. I hope to meet leaders of the main Unions during my year of office. Interaction with politicians, and attendance at political conferences has given me some fascinating and illuminating insights.

All the politicians I met greeted me and treated me with respect. I obtained tickets for party conferences through Christian groups working within the Pprties, with assistance from Ms Rachel Lampard. Rachel was a kind of a "minder" and a mine of information available to me at the Conferences. Newly appointed to her role in the Methodist Church, Rachel also used the opportunities to develop or deepen contacts in political parties. The Christian groups organised prayer meetings, with speakers reflecting on Christianity and politics. Jesuit theologian Frank Reagan was the speaker and I led the prayers at the Liberal Democrats Christian Fellowship; Rt. Hon. Sir Brian Mawhinney addressed the Conservative Christian Forum; and Rt. Hon. Claire Short spoke at the Christian Socialist Movement prayer breakfast during the Labour Party Conference, and urged churches to follow the teachings of Jesus who said "In as much as you do it to the least of these, you do it to me."

Getting a ticket to attend the Conservative Party Conference proved to be most difficult. When I first requested it from the Conservative Christian Forum I was led to believe I would not receive a ticket. "We're a party of Anglicans," I was told. I had already heard that I was considered to be "too left wing" to be given a ticket. "There are Conservative Methodists, " I replied, " and there are Methodist Conservative M.P.s." This argument appeared to carry no weight. "As President I represent all Methodists, and it would be affirming for Conservative Methodists to know that I attended the Conservative Party Conference," I added and then said "the party might recruit more Methodist members as a result of my visit." My arguments proved to be unconvincing. The only reply was "we're a party for Anglicans..... we are predominantly an Anglican party." This conversation took place on 6 July this year, at the Black Majority Churches Conference in Brighton.

I was determined to attend the Conservative Party Conference having made space for it in a busy schedule, and pressed for a ticket. At one point I was sent application forms to apply at the cost of £170.00 for a day ticket. David Ramsden, a political consultant, offered to help me obtain a ticket. I eventually arrived in Bournemouth at 9.45pm on 2 October hoping to attend the conference the next day but still without a ticket. At 11.00pm David Ramsden rang my hosts to say that he'd got a ticket for me! I collected it from David at 8am the next day, and went to the Conservative Christian Forum prayer meeting. At the end of prayers, the man who had insisted the Conservative Party was for Anglicans got up to give notice of a fringe meeting to be held later that day and announced the speakers there would be "Mr Peter Lilley MP, Mr Peter Hitchens a columnist for Daily Express, and the Revd. Prof. Peter Stephens a Methodist minister."

I am familiar with the image of the Conservatives as "Anglicans at prayer". I was reminded at the Liberal Democrats Conference by Mr Alan Beith MP that his party is often described as "Methodists at prayer". I have not heard of any such claims about the Labour Party. However, having been to the conferences of these parties I came away thinking that all three had similarities to the Methodist Conference at least. Style, structures, image and participation appeared disconcertingly similar. In all honesty I have to say though that participants at the Labour Party Conference came closest to representing people I live and work amongst in Sheffield. The platform party on the day I attended the Labour Conference included nine women out of eleven people at the table. It was clear to me that each Party needs to recruit members among younger people, and Britain's black and Asian Communities.

Methodists were well represented at each of the party conferences. I visited all the stalls I could, including those of NCH and MHA. At the Labour Party Conference the NCH stand won the Award for Best Stand. Methodist concerns for children and older people were clearly evident.

My meetings with the Prime Minister and with the leader of the Conservative Party were part of ecumenical church delegations to meet party leaders. The meetings arose out of concerns expressed by the Church of England Bishop Wilfred Woods of Croydon about the language of racism in political campaigns. The delegations sought, and received assurances from all three Party leaders that they would stamp out racist language at local and national level in the forthcoming election campaigns. In the meeting with Mr Hague I also expressed concern that while he would not talk of "bogus" asylum seekers his idea to detain all asylum seekers while their applications were being processed still suggested they were all "bogus". In the meeting with the Prime Minister I acknowledged the presence of a broad minority ethnic representation at the Labour Conference and welcomed the stand made by him there. I expressed concern about a local situation where the placement of asylum seekers had led to community tensions. I asked the Prime Minister how he intended to ensure that his commitment to social and racial justice would be kept at the local level.

The Prime Minister stressed that he was aware that racism was often a "sleeping and vicious dog". He called for partnership between Government and churches to "make racism completely unrespectable and unacceptable". At the end of the meeting with him he said, "keep in touch".

St Paul describes Government as "God's servant for your good" (Romans 13:4 NRSV). We can only have confidence in this by scrutinising government. It has been useful to get close to members of Government and to provoke conversation on what "good" means in relation to different issues. I have held up in conversation the prophetic triple priority of seeking what is good and life enhancing for the elderly, the children and asylum seekers ("the widow, the orphan and the stranger"). These are clear challenges we need to present to politicians in the run up to elections.

Churches need to give attention to, and to watch, God's servants who are politicians and many of whom are Christians. We need to engage and interact with them, seek to understand what is happening in politics, and to monitor political processes. This calls for political astuteness and literacy among church members. This too is necessary if we are to serve the present age, our calling to fulfil. Methodists are making a significant contribution in the contemporary political arena, alongside Christians of other denominations. We all have a part to play in political processes to ensure we have good government, and we must not underestimate the value of prayer in politics.

26th October 2000

Ageing and Nurturing

People in British nations are living longer. Ministry with older people in need has to be a priority today. My cultural background has trained me to respect the elders – older people.

- They are regarded as ones who provided for us when we were dependent on them – and when they are dependent in their old age proper provision must be made for them.
- They are respected for their wisdom accumulated over the years.
- They are respected particularly for their spiritual gifts.
- They are "The Elders".

This cultural upbringing has influenced me all my life, not least in ministry.

MHA has an honoured place in Methodism for holding up the needs, gifts and spiritualities of older people before us all.

This will, and must, continue, and the ideals of MHA will have greater prominence in the next 10-20 years as the numbers of people over the age of 60 increase. I have visited residents in Methodist Homes, and recently opened a Live at Home Scheme at Victoria Methodist Church in Sheffield. New schemes like the Live at Home Initiative are adding to the regular residential care, dementia care and sheltered housing offering support too over 5,000 older people. In addition the spirituality of ageing is nurtured. MHA will have to, and will, rise to the challenges of caring for older people in need from Black and Asian and other cultures with differences in colours, languages, diets and spiritualities.

MHA has to operate in a tough competitive environment in which the needs of individuals have to be considered in the context of Christian principles, ever higher standards and stricter government regulations. Staff therefore are required to be pastoral, professional and prophetic in equal measure. MHA management and staff in all departments include Methodists. Whether Methodist or of other backgrounds the staff are people of great commitment and skill, who care deeply about older people in our society, in vastly complex and demanding situations. Many, lay and ordained, Methodists are voluntarily sharing in the work and providing chaplaincy as part of their discipleship and ministry.

The Bible holds up older people and gives them central place. Many of the

Biblical leaders were well advanced in age, even if it is a young man who has central place, e.g. Sarah, Abraham and Moses.

Here are Biblical stories on which to reflect:

1.   Mephibosheth: 2 Sam 9:1-13

David wished to extend his hospitality to the household of Saul "for Jonathan's sake." He was introduced to Mephibosheth, son of Jonathan who is now aged and quite infirm. King David assures Mephibosheth that he will "always eat at my table". Thus "Mephibosheth ate at David's table like one of the kings' sons." (v. 11) The conclusion of the story is that "Mephibosheth lived in Jerusalem because he always ate at the king's table and he was crippled in both feet. " (v 13)

What lessons and challenges does this story offer as we explore ministry with older people?

2.   Simeon and Anna: Luke 2: 25-28

The Christmas story places a child in the midst. Rightly so. But there is a part of the story that gets sidelined. It is the inclusion of Simeon and Anna in Luke Chapter 2. Both are elderly. Both are clearly respected. Simeon holds the child Jesus, an action that gives much pleasure and affirmation to older people. Anna too comes up to Mary, Joseph and Jesus. The Christmas story focuses on a child, on young parents and on older members of the community.

As you prepare for Methodist Homes Sunday worship and also Christmas, what themes can you weave from these particular stories?

These biblical stories illustrate the respect that is accorded to older people in Scripture. It would be spiritually fruitful, strengthening and illuminating for us all to reflect on them.

Methodist Homes for the Aged Sunday, and Homelessness Sunday are close to each other so we can hold up the needs of those who may be housebound, and those who are homeless. All are impoverished when our care is inadequate, and life is enhanced for us all when we actively engage in mutual respect and care.

2nd November 2000

Roads, Railways and Remembrance

On All Hallows Evening, the night before All Saints Day, I was at Wincobank Chapel in Sheffield. There was a congregation of all ages, but predominantly children. We were meeting to hold before God in prayer, and in remembrance, John Ashton. This young teenager had been killed in a horrible road accident in October 1998. Twelve months ago, on the first anniversary of John's death, we had met and planted a tree in his memory. His death, with all its agony, pain and unfairness, has touched our church community as his life had with all its promise, fun and boundless energy. He laughed at everyone's jokes, and told awful jokes himself; he was cheeky, lovable, irritable, laid back, fragile, like the rest of us. As one of his mates said, "John lived his life to the max." John's funniest joke, that he chuckled over with me, was that I supported Coventry City Football club. I thought it was funny that he supported Sheffield United. Of course the joke was on me when in 1997 Sheffield United beat Coventry City in the FA Cup. John's nickname was Action Man. His sister Jenny has a wonderful picture of him. It was taken during a walk with his friends. All those in the picture have been tramping across muddy moors. John's trousers are covered in mud up to his knees. That's him.

As we remembered John and lit candles, including one made by Jenny, we held before God all victims of road accidents. There are far too many. If you add to them victims of rail, sea and air accidents, we are looking at a global disaster. As many people are killed through such accidents as through gun shootings, yet there is not a great public outcry against this contemporary development.

Petroleum driven traffic adds to air pollution too, and brings a further hazard to all life.

All this sounds a little remote until you start to put names to those who are maimed or killed and the reality is brought closer to home. We remembered John in the context of all victims of traffic accidents.

I remembering John and others we were challenged to:
- drive more carefully, to "kill the speed";
- write to our MPs to support legislation in favour of 20 miles per hour speed restrictions in built up areas;
- reduce our reliance on and use of our cars. Two thirds of our journeys are less than 1 mile long. Shorter journeys are potentially more hazardous not least

because they create more exhaust pollution. Where possible walk that mile That would be better for everyone's health.
- seek improvements to pavements and footpaths;
- express our anger at avoidable crashes.

There is an understandable anger at the Hatfield railway tragedy, and that it had to cost life in this way to push Railtrack into action for safety. Having spent hours on trains recently, my impression, as I returned to Sheffield from Exeter on Sunday 29th October, was that the Railway system was close to total collapse. On three rail journeys in the previous week I had been three to four hours late arriving at my destination. The delays, of course, were attributed to the Hatfield derailment and the ensuing speed restrictions and repairs to railway lines across Britain. Sunday 29th October was described in the News as "the worst day of disruption in the history of British Railways."

Some 20,000 workers were being deployed to carry out repair work on 24 miles of track. Engineers had been brought in from Romania to assist. I was travelling on this day with my two children. Anjuli kept a journal. The delays to our journey were not just due to repair works. Here are some highlights from the journal:

"there will be a further delay ... the lines are being checked because there was a tree on the line..."

"owing to flooding in the Clay Cross Tunnel this train is being re-routed and will have a further thirty minute delay"

At Chesterfield one passenger had to be taken off for hospital treatment

just outside Sheffield station "there is a further delay because someone has pulled the Emergency Cord".

The train was packed out. It was like being on a train in India. I half expected some adventurous passengers to get on and sit on top of the carriages. The train pulled in to Sheffield at 10 p.m., three hours late. It had departed from Exeter on time, at ten past three.

The stormy weather has added further complications. The trains were not just delayed because of leaves on the lines this autumn. Storms have meant that hundreds of trees have damaged lines, and miles of track have been affected by floods.

Passengers have been remarkably patient. Many through have returned to travel by roads again. So road traffic has increased. And the fuel tax protests are set to continue this month.

The whole point of modern travel forms and networks is to give people freedom of movement between places. The reason why the car is popular is that it enables people to travel when they desire, get to places independently, easily, in some comfort, and with speed. I believe we are getting to a point where this dream will be frustrated more and more. There are more and more cars on the road. There are too many cars on the roads. Traffic congestion has increased. A car may have the capacity for great speed, but when it is reduced to snails pace on the M25 or the local road, the frustration is great. Road rage is common. Air rage is not unknown. I've seen rail rage recently. Travellers are heading for frustrations.

More efficient railways, safe and running to time are needed more than ever if people are to move away from reliance on cars. Environmentally and socially this would be more friendly.

At the time of writing, I have heard of another plane crash, two goods trains have collided, and a tanker carrying toxic cargo has sunk near Alderney. In the midst of all the concern that is generated by appalling, often avoidable, accidents, it is important to urge Government and responsible companies to plan for safety before profits. With the need for safety, and protection of environment in mind, I will not be supporting fuel tax protests.

These reflections on traffic and travel have emerged out of the remembrance of John's life and his tragic and untimely death. Some of the congregation assembled at chapel wondered why we were remembering John on Hallowe'en night. We decided it was an appropriate night because it was within the feast of All Saints, and hailed a month noted for remembrance. On 2nd November it was the second anniversary of the death of my mentor, Bert Bissell. The 5th November is Guy Fawkes night. On 6th November is the anniversary of the death of William Temple who inspired twentieth century social responsibility. On the 11th November is Armistice, and remembrance of those who died in World Wars. Also, on the same date, is the anniversary of St Martin of Tours (c.316-397), ex-soldier turned conscientious objector, a monk and bishop. On 26th November we remember Isabella Hardenburgh who was born into slavery in New York. She escaped at the age of thirty. She changed her name to Sojourner Truth and became a traveller to spread God's word, speaking out against slavery.

On 16th November we remember Ignacio Ellacuria who with five fellow Jesuits and their housekeeper and sixteen year old daughter were assassinated by death squads who saw the Jesuit-run University of Central America as fomenting subversion. Ellacuria was outspoken against Government injustice and military atrocities. He had a special concern for "the crucified people", especially the poor. He called on Christians to act to "take the crucified down from the cross."

In your focus on remembrance start with the names of those known to you, and let your remembrance stretch out and embrace those whom you cannot name but whose names are known to God. Whatever it is that crucifies people is an injustice we are called to challenge: war, poverty, hunger, traffic accidents. We hold on to the truth, whether we remember or not, God remembers and longs for the day when the old order will pass and there will be no more death.

9th November 2000

Precision Timing And Many Delays

Delay. This has been the operative word over the last month or so. Delay in many contexts. Sometimes delay and precision come together with resulting amazement, impatience, frustration or pain.

Rail journeys continue to be characterised by delay. Last week I was stranded in London because the Sheffield-London line was shut owing to flooding and track repairs. This meant however that I was one of the first to arrive for a service in Westminster.

It was the first act of worship I have shared in at Westminster Abbey, London. The occasion was a Service of Thanksgiving for the life and work of the Right Reverend and Right Honourable the Lord Robert Runcie, MC. "Visiting clergy and other Religious Representatives" robed in St George's Chapel. Church of England Bishops and clergy robed elsewhere. The Reverend Dominic Fenton, Precentor of the abbey led us to our seats situated in the Lantern. Every seat in the abbey was taken. The service commenced precisely on time at noon.

In the service, Lord Runcie was described as Archbishop and friend, husband and father, who "walked with the great and yet watched for the humble in Church and State". The Preacher was the Bishop of London, the Rt Revd Richard Chartres, who recalled that Lord Runcie spoke for the "Christian conscience" when in a service at St Paul's after the Falklands conflict "his tone was Christian and penitent, rather than triumphalist, as some would have desired." Baroness Thatcher who had been angered by Lord Runcie's sermon at the time was present in the congregation.

The visiting clergy processed back to St George's Chapel. Through glass panels and doors we observed members of the Royal Family greet our Anglican colleagues before departing.

It felt good to represent the Methodist Church and to pay tribute to one who was committed to developing stronger ecumenical relationships. I honour Lord Runcie also for initiating and standing by "Faith in the City" which was rubbished by many as "Marxist" but which subsequently came to be respected for its wisdom. He also launched the Church Urban Fund from which has been donated some £37 million to projects and personnel working with people living in poverty. I have described Lord Runcie as a "cautious" Archbishop, but he clearly demonstrated courage too.

After the service, I had lunch with Baroness Kathleen Richardson and the Rev. Brian Beck. Speaking from experience they enquired, "when are you having your next main meal?" and treated me to a full lunch. This was followed by a lengthy, frustrating train journey back to Sheffield.

My family accompanied me on my next visit to London for the Remembrance Sunday Ceremony at the Cenotaph. Liamarjit and Anjuli had a day with their Auntie, Uncle and cousins while Kathy and I went early on the Sunday morning to the Foreign Office. We drove in our ageing Nissan Sunny along the Mall. No other traffic, but a heavy Police presence. We parked at the back of 10 Downing Street, soon surrounded by limousines, Jaguars, Mercedes Benz and four wheel drives!

Having arrived early we had a leisurely cup of tea alongside those who were gathering to join the various processions. I noticed that some wore white-hearted poppies in memory of the 306 who were shot at dawn for desertion. The white represented white cloth strips that were pinned over the hearts of those who were shot.

We observed representatives of the Merchant Navy arriving, finally allowed to represent seamen who died in the wars. People of all ages were arriving. All wearing poppies and glad to be there. High Commissioners of Commonwealth countries arrived, chauffeur driven, in beautiful cars with striking number plates like FIJ1. Representatives of other faiths than Christian arrived. I felt I was going to be part of a ceremony that was more inclusive than ever before. Remembrance Sunday 2000 was going to be a departure from past ones.

Inside the building Kathy and I were escorted to our various rooms. I joined those who were to process and participate in the Cenotaph ceremony. For half an hour there was time for conversation with most of the forty or so in the room including the Prime Minister, leaders of other Political Parties, some past Prime Ministers, members of the Cabinet, and representatives of "other faiths" (Buddhist, Hindu, Jewish, Muslim and Sikh). A remarkable and unique gathering.

Dr Jonathan Sacks, The Chief Rabbi of the United Hebrew Congregation of the Commonwealth was there. I asked him for a comment on "remembrance". He said, "It is a very important concept in Hebrew Scriptures where it occurs 169 times." He said, "memory is a teacher." I was just going to ask him to distinguish between memory and conscience when Lady Thatcher, who I didn't realise had been listening in, greeted us and the conversation moved on. To be continued...

I chatted with the Chancellor of the Exchequer, Mr Gordon Brown. I thanked him for a positive budget, and for the reduction of VAT on Church Buildings repairs. My main comment to him was about Jubilee 2000 and the relief of Third World Debt. Having thanked him for giving a lead on the issue, I expressed my concern at the delays on the relief of Third World debt, and the need for urgent action. I agreed to meet with him for further conversation, and said that the pressure of Jubilee 2000 campaign would not cease at the end of 2000. To be continued....

I then noted the Rev Ian Paisley, Leader of the DUP, standing alone in a crowded room. I had a question to put to him. After introductions I asked, "What have you done towards peace in Northern Ireland?" Mr Paisley explained that his votes reflected that he was a popular local politician. "But what are you doing to make peace in Ireland?" I asked again. The Rev William Mahood, Moderator of the URC Assembly, came up and introduced himself to Mr Paisley after which I said, "Bill, Mr Paisley was just telling me about his contribution to peace making in Ireland." Mr Paisley quoted the New Testament, "Love thy Neighbour," as he continued. Someone else joined us and the conversation moved on. To be continued.....

Soon we were in a procession, timed to the last second. In turn we all went out into Whitehall. The time keeping was immaculate. As soon as Her Majesty the Queen had taken her position, facing the north side of the Cenotaph, Big Ben struck eleven o'clock. Two minutes of silence commenced.

"Be Still." The Psalmist had requested. This was a request to lay down the arms. The firing of the gun marked the end of the silence, a reminder that the command from the word of God must continue to be proclaimed. The buglers of the Royal Marines sounded the Last Post. Then with prayers and the singing of a hymn, the poppy wreaths were laid.

At the end of the ceremony we processed back indoors. We thus missed the march past of the ex-service personnel and other organisations. Kathy was able to watch this and said it was "a very emotional and moving part of the remembrance service which brought home the human cost of war." It did not feel like a glorification of war.

We had lunch-time refreshments with this remarkable company. Mr Robin Cook, Secretary of State for Foreign and Commonwealth Affairs described the gathering as "truly ecumenical". This was ecumenism in its broadest understanding of the household of God.

Back to London the following Tuesday, for another service in Westminster Abbey, departing at 5.00am for a 10am service, I was still late. Lots of delays on the railways still.

At Westminster Abbey for the Inauguration of the Seventh General Synod, commencing with a Service of Holy Communion and prayers for the Church of England, it was clock-work precision again.

Then on to the Anglican Church House for the Opening Ceremony of the General Synod in the Assembly Hall. The circular hall was packed. Bishops in the centre. Invited Ecumenical guests on the platform. The Archbishop of Canterbury welcomed Her Majesty the Queen and thanked Her Majesty for her "steadfast Christian witness", pledged the loyalty of the Church and then invited Her Majesty to address the Synod. In a brief speech, the Queen spoke of the future of the Church Urban Fund which is closely associated with Lord Runcie; noting the guests of other denominations, she said the continuing search for visible unity was important and mentioned especially the talks with the Methodist Church asking for "God's wisdom to guide them". Her Majesty also hoped for continuing dialogue with the world-wide Anglican communion. The Synod was opened and adjourned for lunch.

A major item for discussion at the Synod according to Papers I had received was a report on the follow up to the Stephen Lawrence Inquiry entitled: "Called to Lead - A Challenge to Include Minority Ethnic People." Our "talks" need to address this alongside affirming women's ministry.

After lunch I headed for the railway station for another delay-ridden journey. On the way I recalled queuing for Holy Communion in Westminster Abbey earlier in the day. Suddenly the line came to a halt. Another line of people was going across. I happened to be at the front of the queue. The Precentor leading us turned to me and whispered, "there will be a short delay."

23rd November 2000

Fish, Chips and Tomato Sauce

"We want a good British meal" - the request of two Brazilian friends who came to stay recently. I wondered which particular British meal they had in mind. "Fish and Chips" was the reply. That's more than a meal. It's a national institution! It could be argued that this meal, more than others, has an impact on the health of England, Wales, Scotland and Ireland in more ways than one. Recent experiences around the Connexion have made me think that this institution is under strain, to the detriment of the health of many, not least in Fishing and Farming communities.

My very first visit to a farm as President drew my attention to rural poverty as a serious issue. That was when I met and listened to Methodist farmer, Mr Eric Johnson, and Mr Clifford Evans of Shropshire Rural Stress Support Network at the Lower Farm in Vennington, Shropshire. Mr Johnson is a dairy farmer. He said, "There were twenty seven milking herds in a three mile radius here ten years ago, and now there are two." Stress levels among farmers are such that there are forty stress management volunteers like Mr Evans working in Shropshire. At present, I pay 33p per pint of milk. The farmer will receive 9p out of that. Mr Johnson said that under these circumstances, if a farm is well managed as a business, it may survive, but small farms are struggling. I saw some falling to bits.

During some time spent in the Plymouth and Exeter District, I took time to visit both cattle and fish markets. One of my teachers here was Mr Alan Andrew, the Methodist Church's Rural Lay Support Worker in North West Devon. Mr Andrew's work allows him space to attend local cattle markets and "to be a listener" to rural communities including farmers. I accompanied him early one morning to the Holsworthy Cattle Market. Cattle were selling at 80p a kilo. Cattle should be selling at £1.00 per kilo according to Mr Andrew. Five years ago the price was £1.25 per kilo. "We have a disaster on our hands," says Mr Andrew, "no one can see what the future is going to be."

It was very easy to chat with farmers at the market. They poured out their concerns. Some farmers are struggling so much that they cannot afford to feed new born calves, so they have to more or less give them away. Some farmers are driven to the point of shooting new born calves. Others cannot bring themselves to do this. It costs a farmer about £25 per week to look after a calf. BSE is an added factor. The sales of beef are down throughout Europe, not just in Britain and France, and the recent rain has either kept cattle indoors or herds have been drowned. I could have stood and listened to the farmers all day. Mr Andrew, and other workers like him, have huge demands on their time. "I go from one case of depression to another," he says.

Alongside the concerns over cattle, meat and milk, the potato crop is failing too. The extraordinary amount of rain is affecting the crop this year. The floods have all but ruined the potatoes, and there are real fears about the crop this season.

It is painful being in a cattle market whether one is vegetarian or not. The cattle look sad. The farmers have glum faces. Very little sign of joy here. A depressing picture all around. Farming is clearly in the doldrums. What is clear to me is that most of the countryside is looked after by the farming communities. If the farmers go out of business, then the countryside of these nations is threatened too. The future of farming is related to the future of the countryside. I asked one farmer what he would like to say to his colleagues, and to me, about this whole situation. His reply was sharp. "Don't get depressed. Get angry!"

The Brixham Fish Market had a similar feel to it. Brixham is a picturesque fishing town. Henry Francis Lyte was Vicar of All Saints in the town and wrote "Abide with me" looking out to the sunset over the sea during the latter stages of his life. Also in Brixham is "Brum by Sea" - the second homes of city dwellers. Some forty percent of homes in such idyllic beauty spots are owned by "outsiders" pushing the prices of homes so high that local born and bred, indigenous, ethnic residents are pushed out of the market.

The fish market is at a low ebb. Fuel prices are having a huge impact on the trade. Added to this are the pressures of fish quotas. The dangers of fishing were brought home to me. The weather conditions and the hours of work involved make fishing one of the most dangerous occupations. There are two deaths per week in the fishing industry in the British Isles, and three boats are lost, on average, every month.

Brixham has a proud fishing tradition. The town has been described as "the mother of fishing," and "the mother of trawl fisheries in England." Alas, this tradition is threatened by the pressures facing the fishing industry today.

Where will the fish, and chips, come from in the future?

A visit to Northbrook Nurseries, Guernsey, was another important experience.

Mr David Faller, who is the grower here put me in the picture. There were 2000 growers on Guernsey not long ago. Now there are just five. The main industry was tomatoes. The industry employed the island community as growers, pickers, packers, sellers and so on. Tomatoes were the topic of conversation. Growers were well off. Then there came competition from Dutch and Spanish tomatoes. The local industry started to collapse. "I used to grow 2 million tomato plants. Now I'm down to 10,000 plants. I am the only tomato grower on Guernsey now."

The finance industry has replaced the tomato industry. People who have come to the Channel Islands as "economic migrants" from the mainland almost outnumber the locals. Here too, house prices are affected. Prophetic voices like that of Methodist Laywoman, Mrs Iris Le Fuerve, ask how the Islands' poor people will be housed - a major concern.

Poverty and stress are real issues in fishing and farming communities. Of course, many are exploring diversification in order to survive. Mr Faller has ventured into growing capsicums, cucumbers and flowers. At Fishleigh Barton Farm, near Exeter, the Methodist owner, Mr Robert Domleo, has opened a delightful country cafe serving delicious home cooking. Some fishermen are going into the provision of bed and breakfast accommodation.

In the midst of all this, small country chapels with declining congregations represent hope and belief. Church members and workers are making an invaluable contribution, giving support to families in crisis. At Church consultations, I have listened to members of Churches express an emerging theology that places creation and crucifixion at the centre, recognising that both represent God's promise of life. Alongside them, the Churches' Rural Resources Centre, based in Stoneleigh, represents Christian commitment to rural communities.

The Government White Paper on the Countryside, published alongside the Government Urban Paper, represents for me the need to see the inter-relationship of rural and urban issues. Emphasis has to be placed on the eradication of poverty, both rural and urban. This requires a comprehensive package of measures, including transport networks and village services such as post offices. As long as farming and fishing communities are not earning money, any expenditure is going to be a problem, whether it is to feed the calves or fuel the vehicles.

I can see the connection between fish and chips and the fishing and farming industries. How was I to relate the Channel Islands to this reflection? The Chair of the Channel Islands District saw an immediate connection: "Tomato sauce!" he said, "Fish and chips and tomato sauce."

When I queued up to collect the "good British meal" at my local chippy in Pitsmoor, I wondered how British this meal is anyway with the various components coming in from other countries. I noticed also that other people in the queue actually ordered "Chips, scraps and curry sauce, please!"

23rd November 2000

God is With Us

"Two thousand years have passed," sang the children at Firs Hill Junior School. The song went on to ask how much more time is needed before poverty ceases to exist. How long will it be before children can be safe?

Danger and threats to the lives of children have been highlighted by the tragic death of Damilola Taylor. The contemporary complexities are seen in the fact that an African child seeking life enhancement in Britain loses his life here. Last year, some 350 children seeking asylum in Britain experienced life in detention centres. Far too many children are excluding themselves from school because it is considered to be an unsafe place and how many of them may be considered to be "educated off-site" by schools?

National Children's Homes (NCH) as a charity, challenges poverty in Britain, as well as other parts of the world, and aims to improve the quality of life of the most vulnerable children. NCH is an important wing in the Methodist emphasis on social justice, and is a leading child care charity. Focused on liberation, empowerment, understanding and respect, NCH's projects for children, young people and families help thousands of people.

In a world in which children continue to face threats to their security, NCH is right to focus on the welfare and well being of children, not least through a commitment to support moves to abolish child poverty. To put a John Wesley spin on it, NCH is there to support children in greatest need, and its golden rule is "to include, not exclude." The work of NCH does make a difference to the lives of children.

According to the United Nations Children's Fund (UNICEF) Annual Report, many countries have to spend more on repayment of external debt than on basic social services. The Report called on world leaders to stop squandering human potential by neglecting the needs of the very young children. Investment in effective childcare makes sound economic sense.

NCH challenges us all to a sustained attack on all the factors trapping children and families in poverty. These include, but go far beyond, issues of income, and include health, education, housing and racism. Much needs to be done to ensure that "opportunity for all" is meaningful for the most vulnerable children as for others.

I was glad to share in the NCH Thanksgiving Service at St John's, Llandudno with the Vice-President who has made her own distinctive contribution to the work of the charity. I have visited a number of NCH projects including one in Dundee, Scotland.

I also visited the place where Damilola fell.

Peckham has a remarkable cultural mix in its communities. This was clear as soon as I stepped out of the London Underground at Peckham Rye, into the main street. This could be seen in the people I saw. The market stalls too reflected cultural diversity in all the fruit and vegetables displayed there. There was a hush in the streets.

Naboth Muchopa, Secretary for Racial Justice, was with me. The Revd. Wesley Daniel, Minister at Peckham Methodist Church, collected us. I asked Wesley first to take us to the spot where Damilola fell and died.

As we drew near to the spot, there was a visible increase in the number of police, and press photographers, camera crew and reporters. The area seemed to be under siege.

A young police woman directed us. It was already dark. We went to the back of a block of flats, and one floor up a dimly lit stairwell. We saw in front of us, by a steel lift door, a collection of flowers. A quiet, lonely spot. Was Damilola brought here? Did he somehow bring himself here to hide, for safety?

We three stood there as visitors. Three dads. In our being, we reflected something of the diversity in communities here, African, African-Caribbean, Asian. A couple of young lads came by. They said, "We live here. It's not as bad as the press makes it out to be. They should leave us alone." Then they were gone.

I looked around. I could hardly believe my eyes. A water leak along a length of the ceiling was bringing out limescale. Stalactites of some 6 - 9 inches had formed. Below them, stalagmites were forming. I banged a finger on these lower formations and noted their solid nature. I have only ever seen such sights in caves. For all the amount of money that has gone into this estate, and we saw the new houses being built, this particular sight demonstrated the extent of hidden urban neglect here. A bright young boy, from a fine family, laid and died here.

This story is a reflection on us all, and is a national shame.

The story of another child will focus our attention as we celebrate Christmas. We will remember as we do so, that this is a painful time for those who mourn the loss or disappearance of a child, those who long for, but know not the pleasure and pain of parenthood.

As I receive Christmas cards and meditate on the images of the Holy Child, born in a stable and lying in a manger, I find it hard not to think of Damilola, lying in a stairwell to die. It is said that the stable in which Jesus was born was in rock formation that was cave-like.

A stable, and a stairwell, neither are good places for the sacredness of birth or death of children. These things do happen, and seem to contradict the Good News that God is with us. Can we discern in the midst of them that God does not neglect or reject places of hardship and is with us at all times and in all places?

Celebrate incarnation - the good news that God is with us.

Remember those for whom Christmas is a hard time, and who feel God is not with them. Let us work with those who seek to ensure that children are safe from all harm.

Shalom.

21st December 2000

Truth and Life In Diversity

In John 14.6 Jesus said ... "I am the way, and the truth, and the life. No one comes to the Father except through me." These words have been chosen to focus Christian ecumenical reflection, prayer and action during 2001, and especially in the Week of Prayer for Christian Unity (18-25 January). Helpful material has been prepared and published by Churches Together in Britain and Ireland to assist Christians. I want to offer some additional material for prayer and action.

Over the last 30 years or so, the words of John 14.6 have been quoted to me more than any other words from Scripture, especially "no one comes to the Father except through me". No one has ever quoted them to me in the context of inter-church relationships. The context has always been inter-faith dialogue and ecumenical relationships with people of other faiths. I cannot come to John 14.6 and ignore this thirty year history.

We live in a world of many Christian denominations. We also live in a world of many faiths. The different traditions of faiths are not a temporary feature of human life. Britain, like other countries, is multi-faith as well as multi-ethnic. Religious diversity is not going to disappear. The Kumbh Mela bringing 70 million Hindus to the River Ganges for a religious ceremony will culminate on 24th January.

There have been church aspirations and prayers to convert all people of the world to Christianity for centuries. Many other faiths are evangelistic too and try to convert everyone, including Christians.

The time has come to acknowledge there is not one faith that everyone will convert to, even though this will remain a hope for many. It is more important to concentrate religious fervour and energy into inter-faith dialogue, and inter-religious co-operation. This would be a great contribution to peace, particularly in parts of the world where different religions compete rather than co-operate over land, territory and space.

In response to comments like these that I have shared in sermons, seminars and lectures, I am always asked, "But what about John 14.6? The Bible says, 'no one comes to the Father but by me'." These words are usually quoted to challenge my views, and also with a hint that they end the discussion.

It is a mistake to reduce "the Bible" to one verse. However, John 14.6 is clearly a verse that requires attention. We have to do some work on this text. An analysis of Biblical commentaries shows that, in the main, there is little comment on this verse. It is almost as if the verse is considered to be a hot potato, best left alone, if controversy is to be avoided. There are those who give reflections. The lengthiest comment is offered by Kenneth Cracknell in "Towards a new Relationship" (SCM, London, 1986. pp.69-107) where he offers a whole chapter on the verse. Read it for yourself.

I believe God is One and enlightens everyone.

I believe people all around the globe have for centuries been responding to the One God's light and self-revelation, and that great histories of response have developed into what we call Religions or Faiths – shaped by different languages, foods, climates, colours, dreams, visions, great messengers of God. Consequently all religions are different.

I believe that the existence of people of many faiths is within God's purposes.

I rejoice in this diversity and thank God for it.

I believe each tradition of faith enjoys special, distinctive and unique gifts, riches and insights. Christians have the life-giving, life transforming story of Jesus as a special gift to share and live by, without arrogance. It is a story by which we can interpret and give meaning to all life. Jesus Christ has been, and is, "the way, and the truth and the life", for millions of people, and will continue to be so for millions.

I believe that people of different faiths should meet with each other, build relationships of respect, and share their faith journey and story with each other. As a result we may all deepen our understanding of God, Jesus Christ and each other.

John 14.6 is not a barrier to this. It is not good practice to quote a single verse without reference to its context in any case.

In John the immediate context places this verse at the centre of a discussion that commences with Simon Peter's question "Lord where are you going?" (John 13.36) and ends at John 14.31 with the words "Let us be on our way".

It is also well recognised that the opening verses of John (1.1-18) offer the key to understanding the rest of the Gospel. Here Jesus of Nazareth is identified with the Word, the Logos (an idea borrowed from Greek wisdom). The cosmic, universal principle and presence (logos) finds physical expression in Jesus of Nazareth. So wherever Jesus speaks or acts we have to see and hear God's action and words. As we read in John 14.10 "I am in the Father and the Father is in me. The words that I say to you I do not speak on my own; but the Father who dwells in me does his works." This is Johannine theology, and suggests that the words "no one comes to the Father but by me" are the words of the Father in Jesus.

God draws people to God's own self, in God's own myriad ways. God speaks to people in many ways, in many tongues. Because God "enlightens everyone" (John 1.9), God is not without witness anywhere. People respond to God in different ways.

For me, John 14.6 is an invitation to Christian ecumenical relationships in the broadest sense incorporating not only different denominations, but different faiths also. This text is an exciting and illuminating gateway to mutually enriching dialogue between different religious traditions.

Loyalty to Jesus goes hand in hand with openness to people of other faiths and the searching challenges they present to Christians. Meet with your neighbours of other faiths, share your faith stories with them. Ask them to share with you their experience and understanding of God. This is an important part of Christian witness today.

Let us lay the foundations for the development of a Council for Faiths Together in Britain and Ireland.

18th January 2001

Life and Clean Air

Does it have to go in the bin? Can it be recycled? Can some shoes, spectacles, clothes be repaired, or re-used? What about good toys that children don't play with any more? Bottles, plastics, foil, cans, cardboard, paper, egg cartons, books – they can be recycled or reused. Perishables can go on the compost. This is a regular topic of conversation in the Bhogal household. Very little goes in the bin. We support the local Green City Action Group. The motivation is primarily respect for the environment.

We live in a Kleenex tissue age. Nothing is meant to last or be kept for long. Things are made to be used and thrown away. There are dangers in this development. In so many ways, even people are treated this way, used and then cast away.

As I share in recycling, repairing and reusing processes I remember a community of people including very young and very old ones who live and work by a rubbish tip in Santa Tecla, El Salvador. Ironically, I had just been to the local recycling banks when I heard on the radio that there had been an earthquake in El Salvador. The report especially mentioned Santa Tecla. My first thoughts and prayers were for the "Basura Community" – the "Rubbish Tip Community" there.

I visited the Community a few years ago while I was in El Salvador for six weeks on a Pastorate Exchange with Baptist Minister the Rev Benjamin Retana. I was accompanied by Noemy, a young member of the Cordero De Dios Church in San Salvador. To reach the Community we walked a mile alongside, and down the Santa Tecla Tip. This tip is not in use any more. It is a very beautiful valley. A stream winds its way through the tip, and along the valley. A community lives at the base of the tip, beside the stream. During a rainy season the stream flooded and carried part of the tip away burying and killing people of the "Basura Community".

Only a strong local protest ensured that all the bodies were recovered, "though there is always someone getting buried in the rubbish", said one resident, "and no one is normally found. The tip is a grave." The people now live in 'safer' spots.

This is a hidden community. It is quite a journey to actually find the people. It is appalling, to say the least, that anyone should have to live or die in these conditions. The people said to me they risk living here for only one reason – LIFE.

Nearby there is another "Basura Community". They are on a tip on the slopes of the San Salvador Volcano. This is an active tip in every sense. It is in use. It is smouldering. Tractors and bin lorries unload and level out the rubbish, adding dust to smoke. Adults and children scavenge in the rubbish alongside hundreds of vultures. People and vultures were fighting, competing for bits of food. We saw waste from hospitals including syringes and needles. "That's waste from a maternity ward", said my companion Noemy. It looked like aborted foetuses or bits of them.

One or two people chatted with us. "I've lived in these circumstances for 15 years. I moved here from the Santa Tecla Tip when it became dangerous …. I am paying for my daughters' education with what I earn here." These are the words of a man who called himself George Harrison. He collected cans into a bag. He would fling bags of cans under a lorry's wheels to get them crushed. "Easier to carry, and I can carry more. I also get more money for crushed cans", he said. Waste merchants pay people like him about £2.00 per day to collect cans, plastics and so on. People on this rubbish tip were salvaging all they could to recycle, reuse or repair. Their motivation – life.

People surround bin lorries, and grab what they can before the vultures, and before the tractors push the loads down the valley. A little girl brought us beads and badges hoping we might buy them. She took a doll and gave it to a weary mum who sat in a cardboard box. Another girl was eating what appeared to be the end of a cornetto ice cream cone. A man was drinking a remaining sip of alcohol in bottle he had just found.

What does all this do to the health of people living in these conditions? What disease and illness is caused by the food and drink found and consumed here daily? How is the dust and smoke affecting people? How many get buried alive without trace? How and why is it that people have to live, work and eat in this way?

As I left, George Harrison said to me: "We get what we can. We work together. We have no fights. We don't rob each other. We don't kill anyone. We don't bother what each other's religious or political beliefs are. We accept each other, and get what we can so that we can have life."

For life, he and others like him live in a kind of Gehenna – a shadowy Hell. This lifestyle is killing them. If they did not try to earn money in this way they would die anyway.

A few days before I visited the "Basura Community" I had sat with Jesuit Liberation Theologian Jon Sobrino at the University of Central America, San Salvador. He said to me that the priority of the Church in El Salvador is "life and clean air". I could see what he meant as I stood in the dust and smoke on a rubbish tip with the "Basura Community".

Not far from the rubbish tips in Santa Tecla some new homes have been built recently for commuters who work in the capital city. The recent earth quake caused a landslide and destroyed some of these homes. At the time of writing some 250 bodies of people have been unearthed. An estimated 1200 people are still missing. The Salvadorian Government has ordered 3000 coffins from Colombia. They are expecting a high death toll. There has been a high loss of life.

The Baptist Theological Seminary, with staff including Carlos Sanchez, and members of the Cordero De Dios Church, have been sharing in rescue and recovery work. Noemy and her mother have had to move out of their apartment in the capital. The whole block is damaged due to the earthquake. Many people are living on the streets fearing aftershocks. Everyone is unnerved.

But what happened to that recycling Basura Community in Santa Tecla? What happened to the other communities living on or near rubbish tips in El Salvador? How many of them were buried alive because of rubbish slips caused the earthquake? I have not been able to find answers to these questions.

I commend the people of El Salvador to you for prayerful support. Don't forget Central America Week 18-25 March with Archbishop Oscar Romero Day on 24th March.

1st February 2001

Mind Your Language!

On 9th January, Kathy was rushed into hospital with what was diagnosed as septicaemia. After a long period of recuperation, Kathy is now recovering and feeling much stronger. We would like to say thank you for all the good wishes, flowers, cards and assurances of prayers that we received at this time. Thank you especially to people in the Liverpool and London South East Districts for your understanding in relation to my engagements and to all who took over additional responsibilities to help support us. We are now hoping that Kathy will be well enough still to go to India this month.

Being at home a little more than usual, I have been able to focus my mind on the visit to India and discuss it with Liamarjit and Anjuli. One of our hopes is that they will be able to see and affirm another part of their heritage, having already visited Nairobi, Northallerton and Dudley. We remembered a story related to a school experience.

Soon after commencing her first school, Anjuli came home one day and said, "Someone called me a half-caste today." I said to her, "You are not a half child. You are fully human, a whole person. You exist through a mum and dad coming together. In your case, because your mum and dad come from two different colours and cultures, you are a doubly blessed child, and you carry within you a double heritage. So you are a richer child. Don't let anyone give you the idea that you are half this or half that. If they do, tell them you have a double heritage."

Some time after this, when Anjuli had five or six of her friends visiting, a remarkable conversation took place. The friends were seated in a circle in our dining room. As they nattered away, one suddenly said, "Did you know 'so and so's' mum has had a baby?"
"It's a half caste," said another.
"No, Not half caste. Double heritage," said Anjuli and explained what that meant.
"Then I'm double heritage too," said the child, "my mother is Welsh and my father is English."
"I'm double heritage," said another, "my mother is Anglican and my father is Roman Catholic."
"I'm double heritage....."

Suddenly, everyone was "double heritage"! A negative concept had been turned into something positive and to take pride in.

But what does "half caste" mean? The 1998 edition of the Concise Oxford Dictionary defines it in these words: "A person whose parents are of different races, especially the offspring of a European father and an Indian mother." I am surprised that a publication that describes itself as "the foremost authority on current English" is still referring to "different races". There is only one human race with all our variety.

Caste is a word formed from (according to the Oxford Dictionary) Spanish and Portuguese CASTA: "lineage, race, breed"; feminine of CASTO: "pure, chaste". The word chaste brings in the concept of sexual purity.

Mulatto is another word worth considering in this context. It is defined as "a person of mixed white and black parentage". The word is formed from the Spanish MULATO which means "young mule" and is an irregular form of MULO "mule".

Mongrel is a word that needs to be mentioned too. The Oxford Dictionary defines this word as "a dog of no definable type or breed" and "any other animal or plant, resulting from the crossing of different breeds or types" but also "a person of mixed race" or "of mixed origin". This word has Germanic roots where it is probably related to "mingle", and takes us to thoughts of racial purity.

Then, of course, there is the phrase "mixed marriage" which the dictionary defines as "marriage between persons of different races or religions". It is that phrase "different races" again. Mixed marriage, in this definition, produces "half castes" and "mulattos".

There is an inherent suggestion in terms like "half caste", "mulatto" and "mongrel" of being only half human, impure and unclean.

The English word "caste" refers to what Hindi or Panjabi calls JATI. An accurate translation of Jati into current English would be "people group" which in Greek is ETHNOS, from which we get Ethnicity. In India there is a deep history of different people groups who have distinct identities and are governed by rules related to hierarchy (VARNA). It is not possible to be absolutely accurate about the origins of this structure among people. Sunil Khilnani, in a book called "The idea of India" (1997, Hamish Hamilton, London) traces it to one of the Hymns of the RIG VEDA within Hindu Scriptures, which describes the dismemberment of the cosmic giant PURUSHA, the primeval male whose sacrifice created the world.

"When they divided the Man, into how many parts did they apportion him? What do they call his mouth, his two arms and thighs and feet? His mouth became the Brahmin; his arms were made into the Warrior (Kshatriya); the thighs, the People (Vaishiya); and from his feet, the Servants (Shudra) were born." The resulting division "defies any simple account," says Khilnani, but, "perplexed Westerners came to describe it by the term "caste". People of different "Jatis" have always lived and worked beside each other in India. But oppressive and degrading rules in relation to purity and pollution have ensured that there is little or no inter-relationship or inter-marriage between them. One particular "Jati" came to be seen as unclean "outcastes" and servants. They define themselves as "dalits", the oppressed and excluded ones. The purity rules of segregation contain the seeds of hatred and animosity. The structures of Jati operate in Indian communities everywhere. All communities go to great lengths to ensure marriage occurs only with one's own Jati. The concept of Jati is bonding within communities and segregating between them. I was brought up with this ideology and have rejected it. Many Indians of all faiths reject Jati and casteism. It is a heresy, no less than any other system of segregation and dominance. I shall explore this a little more with the Christian community in North India.

Christian discipleship has at least two Biblical tools for challenging concepts of many "races" or "Jati" and rules about human impurity. Firstly, the story of creation (Genesis 1) which states that all people are made in the image of God. Secondly, the Body of Christ imagery (1 Corinthians 12) which affirms that all of us, with all our differences, belong equally and are part of one body. These together leave no room in Christian theology for concepts of "many races" or segregation.

If there is one race, language like "multi-racial" or "mixed race" marriage does not make sense. If all are one in the body of Christ, it does not make sense to talk about "mixed marriage" when Christians of different denominations marry each other. The Methodist Conference (2000), in its "Guidelines for Inter-Faith Marriages" does not now use the term "mixed marriage".

So, mind your language! Don't call any person "half caste" or "mulatto" or "mongrel". All people are whole and fully human, and the offspring of all human beings bear the image of God. The language of "mixed marriage" and "half caste" and so on perpetuates the wrong view of races and creates an environment in which people who are different can be de-humanised and attacked. I will never forget the words of a Bosnian "survivor" spoken at the Holocaust Memorial last

57

month. He said that, "when one group of people starts to see another as less than human, that's the beginning of genocide." Resist and break down barriers created between people and human relationships on the basis of race or religious purity. Relationships that emerge from love deserve respect and should be celebrated. All people are children of God and no-one should be treated as anything less than that.

15th February 2001

Embarking on a Journey

Just as I was preparing to set off for India, two good friends died and embarked on another journey. Mrs Nellie Evans of Wolverhampton, and Mr Khan who lived across the road from my home in Sheffield. Both of them died close to the anniversary of my good father's death. I last went to India after he had died there during a visit in 1984.

I met Nellie in 1979 when I went to live and work in Low Hill, Wolverhampton. Polio had severely affected Nellie's capacity to walk.

With her dearly beloved Bill, and then without him, Nellie welcomed me into her home and liked to invite me around for tea. "You sit down and rest while I cook tea", she would say. She always greeted me cheerfully, and showed me great respect.

At a crafts club Nellie made trays and tablemats. The ones she gave me are still in use around our home.

A special memory is that Bill and Nellie came to my Ordination on 1st July 1980 along with a coachful of others from Wolverhampton. The conference was in Sheffield District, and the service was held in Grove Street, Retford. The presiding minister was the Rev Harry Morton. The preacher was the Rev Donald Soper. The lessons were read by Mrs Elsie Moult and myself.

In the sermon Lord Soper asked if anyone had a Rosary. "I have one" he said, "and whenever I struggle for direction I put my hand on my Rosary and invariably I am shown a way forward."

When I returned home to Low Hill after Conference, Nellie asked me around for tea. After tea she sat by me and said, "When Lord Soper asked if anyone had a Rosary I nearly raised my hand and said, 'I have'." Then she held out a Rosary. "I bought this back from a visit to Lourdes and I would like to give it to you as a special gift for your Ordination." I have the Rosary to this day. It is a reminder of Nellie too. It hangs alongside a Mala (prayer necklace) which belonged to my grandfather.

Quite remarkably, I was sharing in worship and preaching in Grove Street, Retford just the day before Nellie's funeral. I was at Grove Street at my own request, as part of my Presidential Pilgrimage to visit people and places that are part of my story. It was great joy to be there, and to recall my Ordination. I shared the story of Nellie Evans with the congregation.

Mr Khan died very suddenly though he has been poorly all the six years I have known him and his family. We had frequent conversations about God, or, to use the Arabic term, Allah. He often brought food across the road to share with us, and always at festivals like Id. He was a good neighbour. He was the one who constantly reminded me that it is not possible to be a Muslim without a deep respect for Jesus.

I attended Mr Khan's funeral which took place at 7pm. It was preceded by one of the five prayers of the day. It seemed so right and natural that a funeral is linked to a regular act of worship and prayer. The ceremony took place in a former Methodist Church Hall, adjoining Firth Park Methodist Church, Sheffield. A Methodist congregation are the neighbours. What is it to be neighbours as Methodists and Muslims?

The hall is beautifully decorated with wall to wall carpet on the floor. It was packed for prayer. I was so impressed and thrilled that so many had gathered for prayer, and not for the first time in the day.

The worshippers stand facing east in straight rows, with spaces between them. The whole body is used in prayer in cycles of movements, adopting postures of standing, bowing, kneeling and sitting.

I observed from the back of the hall.

I recalled the words of God to Ananias (Acts 9) and especially the phrase "he is praying" (Acts 9:11). There is something profoundly disarming and inspiring about observing people in prayer.

I could not join the prayers. But as I sat in the hall I was pleased to see it in use as a House of Prayer. As the people prayed Allah Ho Akbar (God is great), I said in my own prayers God is good, God is great, Alleluia, Praise God. And I gave thanks for Mr Khan. Out of respect for my attendance, Mr Khan's elder son chose to sit and say his prayers with me at the back.

My father died on a visit to India. He had gone alone. I accompanied my mother to collect his ashes and to scatter them in a river.

Before going my mother asked me to take her to her "Guru". We went to a Sikh Gurdwara (Temple). While she went to wash her hands I waited. I noticed others arriving and going with their concerns into one particular room where the Guru sat. One man who went by had no arms or legs. I reflected on my own suffering in the context of the pain of others. My mother and I went into the room, it was packed. Numerous people were waiting for an audience with the Guru. When the Guru heard my mother was there he sent for her. They were friends from village childhood. We jumped ahead of the queue, and went into a small room. I saw there, on the floor, on a rug, the man who had no arms and legs. I discovered he was physically blind too.

I was amazed that people in pain and hardship brought all their burdens to share with a Guru such as this. He comforted my mother. He was delighted to meet me, and knew of me by reputation. He asked me about church and ministry, and where I lived. He described the Manse as SACH KHAND (the House of Truth). Sach Khand is the name normally reserved for the home of the Word of God (Truth).

As I sat before the Guru I reflected on the words of the prophet Isaiah

> *"... he had no form or majesty that we should look at him .... a man of suffering and acquainted with infirmity ... "* (Isaiah 53: 2-3)

The man in front of me reflected the image of God no less than anyone else. I felt I saw in him a vision of the suffering servant of God. I will never forget him.

My encounter and conversation with the Guru had a profound effect. The respect he showed me invited the same from others. In my experience this culminated in the moment when my sister and mother came on the Conference platform in Huddersfield and presented me with a ROMALA, a cloth normally used to hold the Word of God. It was a symbol of the respect for me, and a way of saying, hold up the truth.

I called my father, Pita Ji (Dear Dad). In Sikhism God is also referred to like this: Tu Hi Mera Pita, Tuhi Meri Mata: You are my father, you are my mother. The term people use to refer to Dad, is the term used to refer to God. It is like the Hebrew term Abba, Father. Jesus referred to God as Abba. Sikhs as well as Christians call God Father. This illumination makes us think a little more about the words "no one comes to the Father but by me" (John 14:6).

8th March 2001

61

The Lord Provides a Table

Rubble surrounded by the Desert of Kutch. There's been a drought in the area since 1997. A cyclone hit the coastal area on 9 June 1998. On top of all this a devastating earthquake came. It flattened most buildings with not one brick left standing on another. Every building and every body in the area has been affected. The effect of one minute when the earth shook, buildings "rocked like boats", and every heart trembled. This is the Western region of Gujarat, close to the India-Pakistan border. Mounds of rubble everywhere. Ironically, Kutch derives from the Sanskrit for fatal waste. The precise death toll in this disaster will never be known. Locally people are talking in terms of 100,000.

The earthquake rocked Gujarat on 26 January, India's Independence Day. Parties and processions were in place all around the country. In Anjar, close to the epicentre of the earthquake, four hundred children and fifty teachers died at a gathering in one school when the building collapsed.

When I heard about the earthquake, I had to look at a map to see where Bhuj, also by the epicentre, was. I made up my mind to visit the city during my visit to India, and spent the last two days of the trip there. I travelled from Delhi to Ahmadabad by plane, followed by a 400-kilometre drive by car to Bhuj.

I was met in Ahmadabad airport by the moderator of the church of North India, the Rt. Rev. Z J Terom, the Deputy Moderator, the Rt. Rev Malakar, and the Bishop of Gujarat Diocese, the Rt. Rev.V. M Malaviya. The four of us made a visit to the Kutch region together. Bhuj is the furthermost city in the Diocese, close to Pakistan. It is well and truly off the beaten tourist trail.

Bhuj did have a population of some 150,000. It is described in the India Guidebook as "picturesque". The city is overshadowed by the Bhujia fort, remains of which are still visible on a hill.

Forty kilometres outside Bhuj, the reality of the earthquake began to be apparent. Large cracks in the roads and in the ground. Bridges damaged though still in use. I was greatly distressed to see crowded busses and heavily laden trucks still speeding across these. We came to the town of Bachau, a word that in Hindi means "to save". The town is reduced to rubble. My first sight of the utter devastation of the region. A man was carrying a child whose arms and legs and head were in bandages. Blue or white tarpaulin tents represented the only inhabited dwellings. Every building is out of use. Some larger tents sheltered relief camps. People are out in the open. There was an atmosphere of silence. Everyone was busy, some breaking larger collapsed walls, others carrying away rubble which is mostly being deposited alongside highways. The poorest who live off scraps where collecting and breaking metal rods out of concrete. There were small food stalls. A chair with a mirror propped up in front – the hairdresser's base.

Here or there are one or two people sitting on mounds of bricks that made home so recently. Bishop Malaviya pointed to a grey clearing in the midst of fallen buildings. "That's the area for burning bodies", he said.

In Bhuj my hosts took me straight to St Andrews church in the centre. The building, 170 years old, is still standing but it is now on unsettled ground. There are large cracks in the structure. Tiles have fallen off the roof, as has the bell. The building will have to be demolished. We shared in a short act of worship in this broken place. A congregation of 50 or so, with evidence of pain in their whole being, sang praise to God. They have lost loved ones, homes, and livelihood.

One young woman, aged no more than eighteen or nineteen sat in the back row, her head covered in a red sari. She was holding a child aged no more than nine months or so. One or two other people sat beside her. The woman appeared to be practically hiding herself.

At the end of the worship, the four visitors were garlanded with marigold flowers. Wherever I smell the fragrance of the marigolds I will be back in Bhuj.

Then I assisted with the distribution of the relief supplies to the gathered people. Cooking stoves and pots, tents and money were shared out. The Church is also working through Churches Auxiliary for Social Action (CASA). The Methodist Relief and Development Fund is assisting through CASA. When the woman in the red sari came to receive her provisions she was introduced to me as one who had been married less than one year. The house she had just set up with her husband had been demolished in the earthquake. Her husband had pushed her and the baby out of the house but the house was down on top of him, in the doorway, before he could get out. He was crushed under the bricks. She has a gorgeous baby called Pretty.

At the close of the visit to the Church, some of the worshippers took me to see the remains of their homes. Each one took me to a pile of bricks. A Doctor showed me his broken home, then he took me to the tent where he is now living, and pointed to an area cleared of rubble. He said, "That's where I worked in the Bhuj General Hospital that stood there." Every patient receiving treatment on 26th January died when the building collapsed. The surviving Hospital Staff now assist with the treatment of injured people in a medical tent.

We left Bhuj and travelled on. Every town and village is just rubble. Ratnal Town is rubble. Anjar is flattened too. We went to Gandhiham, described as a town of industry and agriculture, and of hotels and high rise buildings. Every building here is damaged or demolished. The Hotel business is reduced to nil.

I attended another Church service here and assisted with the distribution of relief supplies. Night came. As we sat and rested, we felt aftershock tremors. "The tremors come every two to three hours," I was told.

A group of teenagers sat by me and described how the earthquake felt. "We thought a war had started and that bombs were rocking the area, or that a nuclear bomb had gone off. The rocking lasted for one and a half minutes. We just stood and prayed. When the rocking stopped, we noticed that buildings had gone." This fortunate group had been standing in a school playground.

I asked one older member how the earthquake had affected his life. "I've lost everything. My family, my house, my business." He later explained that he used to sell chickens. Now he can't. His customers were the hotels which are now all gone. "Are there not other customers?" I asked. "Others can't afford the chickens," he said. "What about wealthier people," I asked. He said that they had left the area after the earthquake. "I can't sell the chickens and I have no seed to feed my chickens," he said, "I can't buy seed if I don't have money. I don't have money if I don't sell the chickens. So I have given the chickens away. I'm finished." The Church is now assisting him to build up his life again. He has a tent, two chickens and some money to feed himself and the chickens. But when will he have customers?

I stayed overnight in Gandhiham. The four visitors were given shelter in a single storey home that was still standing though cracked. There were tremors all through the night and I wondered if the building would collapse over us. In the morning my host asked me how the night had been. "Fine," I said, "what about you?" The reply was, "I didn't sleep. With you four under my roof I could not. I had to stay awake just in case I needed to rush you out." It has become clear to me that many people in the area now prefer to sleep in the afternoons, out in the open.

While I was in this earthquake area, I heard about the earthquake in Seattle. 100,000 were killed in Gujarat, only one died in Seattle. Why? One reason may be that houses in Gujarat were not built as securely as in Seattle.

There has been a huge response to the earthquake in terms of providing relief. The primary challenge is co-ordinating it, and ensuring that everyone, especially the poorest, receives assistance. As a result of our visit, the Church of North India (CNI) has committed itself to rebuilding one whole village with all the necessary infrastructure. Churches in Britain may be able to work in partnership with CNI in this work.

I flew out of Bhuj Airforce Airport, which itself has been affected. My abiding memory of this visit will be the first thing that happened when we arrived in Bhuj after a five hour drive. We went to the Church. A community had gathered to welcome us by washing our hands and giving us a meal and a glass of water. We sat out in the open to eat. I looked around and saw the remains of this desert town, with the broken fort on the hill. I was amazed and inspired by the spirit of people who have lost everything and who, from somewhere, produced a most beautiful meal. I recalled the words of the Psalmist: "Can the Lord provide a table in the wilderness?"

15th March 2001

Borders and Binoculars

Binoculars to my eyes, from a hideout, I looked over the India-Pakistan Border at Khem Karan in Panjab. I could see people, though I could not make out their features. An odd experience. Most of my neighbours in Pitsmoor, Sheffield, are of Pakistani origins.

At the Wagha Border point near Amritsar, a spectacular Indian and Pakistani military performance shows how strongly borders are preserved and defended. Where there are gates, there are gatekeepers to hinder or allow a carefully observed and monitored crossing. Some of our Group crossed the border and stepped into Pakistan briefly under the watchful eye of the gatekeepers.

The India-Pakistan border was drawn in just 36 days in August 1947 by Sir Cyril Radcliffe without travelling anywhere near the area.

The border area is very beautiful. It includes Kashmir, Panjab and Kutch, and remains a matter of dispute to this day. Hindus, Muslims, Sikhs and Christians live in uneasy tension. The testing of nuclear weapons recently by India and Pakistan has heightened tension.

A visit to India had been on our family agenda for 15 years. Kenneth Wilson of "Soul of India Tours Ltd" heard me talking about this, and the result was that we and 26 others made the journey. It became an opportunity to join the President of Conference on a Pilgrimage of "A Christian Exploration of the Sikh Faith in India".

Some members of the Group had been to India or Pakistan before. For others it was a whole new experience. For all of us it was a unique experience in which we explored borders and boundaries, not least in terms of faith and spirituality.

India has a population of one billion, and offered us a million images each day. The population increases by 18 million each year. It is not easy to get away from people and sound. Yet the gift of India is the art of solitude and deep inner stillness in the midst of crowds and noise.

We visited the Taj Mahal, a marble monument to love. Rabindranath Tagore defined it as "a tear on the face of eternity" that echoes the cry "I have not forgotten, I have not forgotten, O beloved" (The Flight of Swans). The Taj evokes love and romance. There is an interplay of the boundaries of dreams, fantasies, realities, pain and pleasure here.

We spent time in the bustling city of Delhi, but India lives in villages. There is breathing space in villages. The fields are green, water supply is plentiful. India is fed from the food grown by the villagers of Panjab. We glimpsed something of this when we visited the villages my mother and father hail from, Dhanowali and Kotli Than Singh. In Kotli we were welcomed and fed by some of my relatives. The village has grown considerably since I was last there, it is practically a small town. In another place Liamarjit and Anjuli enjoyed milking the cows and buffaloes. We noted that animal feed is a fresh, green supply of fodder.

We travelled to Amritsar, the second largest town in Panjab, and is the home of Harmandir Sahib, or the Golden Temple, the holiest Sikh shrine.

Thirteen members of the Group visited the Golden Temple for prayer in the "ambrosial hours" of the morning, between 3am and 6am. A procession brings the holy scriptures, the Guru Granth Sahib, into Harmandir Sahib, which is surrounded by a large pool of holy water (Amrit, from which the sanctuary gets its name). A constant flow of pilgrims follows the route of the procession to pay homage, to worship, to make offerings and receive Kara Prashad (sacrament). It is an inspiration to observe people of all ages, including infants, make this prayer pilgrimage while it is yet dark. I reflected that the practice of prayer early in the morning is part of Methodist heritage.

In the daylight hours we visited Jalianwala Bagh, the site of the most brutal massacre under the command of General Dyer in 1919. This visit was a painful experience for our Group, bringing most to tears.

The whole group spent time together at the Golden Temple, and accompanied me when I met the Supreme Sikh Leader, Mr Joginder Singh, known as "the Jathedar". He stated the core of Sikhism and the challenges facing Sikhism. I asked him to comment on Christian perspectives like Jesus is God Incarnate, Jesus is uniquely the Son of God and the words attributed to Jesus in John "no-one comes to the Father but by me." He stated his view without in any way ridiculing or undermining the views of Christians. There were about fifty people, including the Bishop of Amritsar, the Rt Revd Samantaroy, in the room when this conversation took place. I felt exhilarated and exhausted after this engagement. The meeting had been organised by Mr Daniel Das, a CNI Layworker whom I met when he came to study at Kingsmead College, Birmingham in 1982.

The next day we went to Baring College, Batala, where Prof. Clarence McMullen has developed a resource for Sikh-Christian Dialogue. He and Mr Daniel Das had organised a Day Conference for us on "The Status of Women in Religion: Theory and Practice". The Conference began with prayers led by representatives of different faiths including me. The speakers were three women and three men, including the Vice President. The Conference provided a useful platform to share insights from different faiths. There was heated debate over the view that there is an inbuilt bias against women in all faiths. The final statement of the Conference recognised that gender bias and oppression of women has been sanctioned by all religious traditions and that there is a need to stand in solidarity with each other as women and men. All faiths, in theory, call for equality of women and men. It is in the practice that there is inequality.

In all these experiences, we stood on many frontiers with people from different backgrounds. The boundaries that we explored have, in many cases, been drawn by others, on our behalf, from a distance. The India visit demonstrated the need for us to stop peering across divides through binoculars from distant spaces. We need to meet face to face, flesh to flesh. Such encounters can be costly, not least in terms of time and effort, but can be enriching.

Borders have a place. Where we have invitation and opportunity to cross them, we are beckoned to travel a little further on journeys of exploration. When we meet as good neighbours we do not need binoculars.

29th March 2001

"I Stand At The Door And Knock"

Migrant Helpline at the Eastern Dock in Dover Harbour deals with 40-50 people wanting to enter the UK by this route each day. On the office walls, and in the Chaplaincy room, hang calendars showing Holman Hunt's portrayal of Jesus Christ as "The light of the World" with the quote from Revelation 3:20: "I stand at the door and knock". The door Christ is knocking on appears to be one that has not been opened for a long time. It is covered in weeds and thorns. The despairing look on his face suggests that Christ has no hope of the door being opened. The door is meant to be a door to the human soul. It is illuminating to reflect on this in the context of immigration and asylum. I saw this painting again when I was in the chapel at Rochester Prison during a visit to asylum seekers. I sat just below this painting as I asked officers why asylum seekers are locked up in a conventional prison.

The Gospel perspective on immigration is that we see Christ in the ones who stand and knock at the doors of our nations. We see Christ in asylum seekers who are detained in our prisons and who knock on those prison doors. The doors can be opened.

The technical word for these doors is 'borders'. I have written (Methodist Recorder, 29.3.2001) that borders have a place. This is particularly the case where borders protect the most vulnerable from being overpowered and abused. In terms of contemporary immigration and asylum in Europe, borders exist lest the vulnerable should overwhelm those with power and privilege. Where that is the case, the injustice of borders should be challenged.

Immigration and asylum legislation in Britain has been tightened over the last thirty years or so to the point where the doors are effectively closed. A person simply seeking to enhance life through participation in the UK cannot do so. It is not possible to arrive legally in the four nations of the British Isles and to seek refuge here. People are, therefore, left to take subversive routes across the borders. They hijack planes; stow away in containers, living in them for weeks; sail the seas in sub-standard boats; ride under trains; hold on to the wheels of jumbo jets in flight. Countless numbers get killed in the process of seeking a better life. Some people make a living out of the criminal activity of human trafficking. Legal routes are shut. People try to get around them by applying for political refuge or "asylum".

When people are left to take such desperate measures to escape poverty or persecution, the media exploits the stories. An impression is given that millions of people are making their way to Britain; that they are only heading this way because Britain is seen to be a "soft touch"; that this already overcrowded little island will be overwhelmed if the doors are opened, "Why don't they go to other countries?" people ask. Such fears are used by some politicians also to seek further restrictions or "deterrents" in immigration and Asylum laws. The Conservative Party has said that those who come through the nation's doors uninvited should be imprisoned.

Some 1000 people are currently held in detention centres "awaiting removal". A voucher system means that there are no cash benefits for those awaiting the outcome of their "asylum" applications. "Asylum seekers" are seen as a drain on the nation's resources, a burden on the tax payer and as "illegal immigrants". Thus they are criminalised, and become easy scapegoats for all ills, and targets of attack or abuse.

Our immigration and Asylum laws, and media coverage of stories related to them, give some of the clearest expressions of racism (exercise of prejudice and power in dominating and destructive ways). A Council of Europe report published last week was very critical of the racism encountered by Asylum Seekers and Refugees in Britain, as well as in other parts of Europe.

In February, the Home Secretary Jack Straw reported that, two years on from the publication of the Stephen Lawrence inquiry report, more than 70% of the recommendations had been implemented. The Council of Europe's report had picked up on some of this, especially in relation to policing, and said some favourable things, but it noted that there is a long way to go yet.

For one of the clearest indicators of where we are at any time in terms of the achievement and attitudes in relation to racial justice take note of what happens in relation to immigration and asylum issues. Clearly we do have a long way to go. Churches of all denominations have spoken out against the injustices in our immigration and asylum processes. They have taken action denominationally and ecumenically.

I have met with Barbara Roche, the minister for immigration, as well as with the Home Secretary and the Prime Minister to share some of my concerns, and the concerns of the Methodist Conference on these matters.

As indicated in my address to Conference, I have pressed for new immigration and asylum laws which recognise the multi-cultural, multi-ethnic identity of contemporary Britain and which are created through international partnerships. Borders are quite recent creations. Can we live without them? Can they be blurred?

What do you think? What vision does Christian discipleship have to offer about immigration and asylum? Barbara Roche has asked for assistance from us.

Churches have much to offer. I want to invite Methodist members to share some reflections. Here are a few jottings from me to get the ball rolling, and I will offer a little more in my next column.

The Bible contains stories of a travelling people of God, and suggests that God's first instructions to people were words like "fill the earth" (Genesis 1:28; 9:2), and "Go from your country...to the land that I will show you" (Genesis 12:1).

Egypt is remembered mainly as a place of oppression, but it was also a place of plenty and security. The children of Jacob headed that way when there was grain in Egypt (Genesis 42:2), and the Holy Family fled to Egypt when they were in danger (Matthew 2:14). These are stories of "economic migrants" and refugees.

Christian ministry is about opening doors. The chains and locks on the doors have to be loosened. The result is, in the words of Revelation 3:20 "I will come in ... and eat with you, and you with me."

12th April 2001

"You Welcomed Me"

The stranger who joined the disciples on the road to Emmaus is only recognised as Christ as they shared food. "When he was at the table with them, he took bread, blessed and broke it, and gave it to them. Then their eyes were opened...." (Luke 24:30-31). We read the words of Christ, "When I was a stranger, you welcomed me." (Mt 25:35)

Giving hospitality by sharing food and shelter is a consistent theme in the Bible. In the midst of all the stories of conflict and animosity, we read of people who took sanctuary and received protection in cities and homes. In particular, the prophets held up the needs of "the widow, the orphan and the strangers." In the contemporary world the prophetic edge requires the welfare of children, older people and the refugee. I have already written about children and older people. I am focusing here on the refugee.

People do not talk about refugees so much as of asylum seekers today. Article 1 of the 1951 United Nations Convention on Refugees defines a "refugee" as someone with a "well founded fear of persecution" seeking protection. If that defines a refugee who is an asylum seeker? Is an asylum seeker a refugee? Are applications for refuge or asylum considered on the same criteria? The Amsterdam Proposals, a new European Directive on asylum, certainly recommends this. If this is the case, we do not need the term "asylum" in matters of immigration. There are refugees who seek protection from persecution. What we need to do is to broaden the definition of persecution to include the fact that there are economic as well as ideological or religious threats to people's lives. Poverty terrorises and uproots people too and forces then to seek protection for their lives. Refugees should not be called "asylum seekers".

The term "asylum seeker" should be dropped. People do not seek asylum. Asylum is given. The term asylum has a historical use and connotation. It has been used to refer to institutions giving shelter and support to people suffering from mental illness who were considered to be a threat to society. Such places, where people were placed and forgotten about, belong to a bygone era. Such a use of the term is discontinued. It smacks of degradation and indignity. Why use such a term to refer to people desperate for the protection of their lives?

The term "asylum seeker" has been so abused that its use now criminalises people. It has become synonymous with "illegal immigrant".

Bearing in mind the ever strong tide of xenophobia and racism in Europe, these countries need to move beyond new proposals on asylum, and to create new and welcoming approaches to the freedom of movement and immigration. We need measures that promote diversity as a value for society as a whole. European governments need to lead by example and demonstrate how to integrate, reflect and enhance diversity.

Freer movement of people will not mean that millions of refugees will "flood" into Europe. The majority of the world's refugee community takes shelter in the poorest countries of the world. European nations, with all the wealth they represent, should be more welcoming and hospitable to refugees.

In the short term, Europe needs to welcome people who need protection and security. In the long term, Governments need to act internationally to create good development strategies which will help people feel safe and fulfilled in their own homes. For this, they need to end debt, eliminate poverty, stop the arms trade, and bring ethnic cleansing and killing to an end.

There are approximately 1,500 "asylum seekers" who are being held in captivity in detention centres and prison. I have visited the five largest centres at Haslar (Gosport), Tinsley (Gatwick Airport), Campsfield (Oxford), Harmondsworth (Heathrow Airport) and Rochester Prison. I hope to visit also Lindholme (Doncaster), Oakington (Cambridge) and McGilligan's Prison (Northern Ireland). All these centres have significant locations, often close to ports of entry or exit. Harmondsworth nestles amongst 5 star hotels.

I started my visits to "asylum seekers" at Haslar near Portsmouth. I arrived by ferry at Gosport Harbour, home to Haslar Marina, holding luxury yachts owned by multi-millionaires. A sign here likens Gosport to "God's Port, our Heaven". For the detention centre I had to follow the signs to "HMP Haslar".

The detention centres and prisons vary in standards in terms of conditions and provisions. They all have the appearance of prisons. Perimeter walls and fencing of 18 feet, all of them supporting razor blade crowns. All the centres I visited were full to capacity with people mainly from Eastern Europe, but also from Middle Eastern, Asian and African countries. There were up to 40 different languages present, with translations either non-existent or provided by those who were held. Translators are available but not readily so.

Most of those I met were young people, all of them separated from their families.

My itinerary did not allow space to have in-depth conversations. I had to do much of the talking in corridors as I passed by, or at the end of worship in "Chapels" or "Mosques". From these conversations I can say that the young people felt isolated, vulnerable, lonely, weary, depressed, angry, traumatised and shattered by the ridicule, suspicion and hostility they had experienced in Britain. Many of them are from zones of conflict and have experienced torture, imprisonment, the abuse or loss of their families and homes. Research currently in process indicates that over half have suffered at least three such traumas. I met one or two people who had just been brought into captivity; their whole being showed the fright of a fish just hooked and brought out of water. I felt the anger of one of them who described his experience as torture, because he had just been separated from his wife and young child. One was still in shock at what was happening to him and hardly able to speak. Both of these young men have been living in Britain for some time. They would be termed "overstayers". To be separated from family is inhumane nevertheless. I asked as many as possible why they had been detained. Not one could give me an answer. When I asked how long they had been imprisoned in this way, the answers ranged from 1 day to 2 years. When I asked if they knew how long they would be detained, the answer in every case was, "I don't know." A person is informed verbally as to the reasons for detention, but nothing can be grasped or understood by someone in the shock of sudden loss, and language may be a barrier too.

When I asked the governors or other senior staff if they knew why people were being held, none of them had any answers either. "We do not know automatically why people are detained. We do not have specific reasons", said one. Another person said, "We do not need to know. We just provide a service for the Immigration Office." Immigration officers at ports make decisions for those arriving without entry papers, granting some temporary admittance while their case is processed, and sending others for immediate detention. Increasing numbers are being detained on arrival.

The uncertainty in the circumstances places huge pressures on the mental, physical and spiritual health of those detained.

There is ecumenical and inter-faith chaplaincy service to "asylum seekers" in detention. I have wondered whether Churches should be supporting detention of "asylum seekers" by providing chaplaincy. I asked what chaplaincy is for in such contexts. Those who are detained and staff find companionship and strength from chaplains. Many look forward to worship and prayer. There is an opportunity for theological reflection on the experience of detention. Chaplains provide a listening ear at a critical time, and keep a watchful eye on the treatment of those detained. Worship is energetic, not least in the hymn singing. I heard a forthright sermon from one who had been detained for 7 months. The basic theme was that Britain is spiritually impoverished: this can be seen from its treatment of the most vulnerable, and "when we come out we will preach the word of God to change the nation, and be a blessing here."

I brought a short message in the context of worship on the theme of Jesus' unjust arrest and imprisonment, based on words (from Mark 14: 43-65), such as "many witnesses told lies against Jesus, but their stories did not agree" (Mark 14: 56). I suggested Jesus' story might give some meaning to their experiences. It was received with loud "amens".

There are matters here that cause me serious concern. Governors tried to make it clear to me that those detained in connection with "asylum" are not treated as prisoners. But, as the Vice-President Sister Eluned Williams said to me after one visit, "Whatever they say, it's a punishment". Detention is imprisonment. Officers and other staff have a prison mentality. "Why are we in prison when we have committed no crime?" is a question I have been asked consistently by those detained. Rochester is a conventional prison. People in the detention wings here told me that they had been kept locked up for up to 19 hours a day. This is wrong and inhumane.

I was surprised to find that, apart from one centre, staff, including chaplains, in detention centres are barely representative of those detained. The same goes for volunteer visitors. In fact, the only black or Asian people present were those detained. One worker in a detention centre said to me and my colleagues, "50% of the staff here are very good, 25% are bad, 25% are very bad, towards those who are detained." There is an assumption of criminality here. "Asylum Seekers" are considered as fraudulent and not genuine. One prison officer said, "The majority of them are economic migrants, but we do not make any judgements...they cost the tax payer a fortune." The same officer talked to me and the Vice-President about where these prisoners are "fed" and where they are "walked" as though he was talking about some animals. We were also given the impression that work in detention wings is unpopular among officers. They would rather not do it.

I have many concerns about the imprisonment of "asylum seekers" who fall foul of the immigration and asylum legislation. The use of prisons like Rochester and Haslar should be discontinued. The use of detention centres should be phased out as soon as possible.

One group of volunteer visitors has said to me: "As we visit detainees week by week, we watch them lose their enthusiasm for activities on offer, become passive, depressed and sometimes suicidal.   Although psychological and psychiatric help is available, it is unable to cope with the scale of the demand. Government is hoping to treble Britain's detention beds by the end of 2001. Detention may be necessary in a few cases, but we do not feel it is a humane, economic or even effective way to deal with Britain's immigration problems." Detention has not been a deterrent.

26th April 2001

Learning and Location

"We'll make a Minister of you," said members of Low Hill and Fordhouses Methodist churches soon after I arrived there as a "green" young whippersnapper of a probationer! I had just spent four years in "theological education" at Hartley Victoria College and Manchester University. In Wolverhampton, I was re-trained for ministry in that particular context.

In my experience of ministry, I have found that local congregations I have served with have been the location and centre of my continued learning and training. Theological education equipped me with some key foundation skills. I have been formed and re-formed for ministry by those I have worked with.

Ministry has required different styles in different contexts. What has remained consistent is the need to reflect Jesus' priorities: to be committed to the poor, identifying and eating with those on the margins of society, and expressing respect to those of other faiths and cultures. Added to this, in each context and with each set of premises involved, it has been necessary to spend considerable time and energy on buildings.

I have always valued opportunities for further training, and have benefited from some available "Connexionally". Being President has been a fantastic learning experience. I will be able to take this into my continuing role as Director of the Urban Theology Unit (UTU) and minister with Upper Wincobank Undenominational Chapel within the Sheffield Inner City Ecumenical Mission.

I have been able to visit all but one of our theological training 'colleges'. It has been a pleasure to share my vision for the church and for the nations with Foundation students and those training for diaconal and presbyteral ministry. The "colleges" and "courses" available regionally represent an important resource for the development of the whole church, and most of them now function ecumenically. I wished to visit them as an expression of solidarity as President of Conference, and as an expression of my commitment to relevant theological education and training.

The challenge facing theological education and training is to provide resources to equip the whole people of God for ministry, mission and worship in a changed and changing context of the twenty-first century. For that we require basic knowledge, key skills and deep wells of spirituality. An essential personal quality required in those selected for diaconal, lay or presbyteral ministry is "trainability", an openness to listening and learning.

We need such education and training, and as a priority must fund it adequately, and ensure it is accessible to the whole church, young and old, women and men, black and white, and all of us with our range of abilities and disabilities.

Sheffield Synod meeting last month gave an assent to almost £4 million's worth of property schemes in the District. I'm sure other synods will have had similar schemes at similar levels of funding. These levels of funding for property schemes are undertaken because seventy-five per cent of our buildings are now over 100 years old, and require attention. Synods are able to give assent to such schemes with some enthusiasm. We need equal vigour to raise funding for theological education and training. Otherwise we will be left with fine, empty buildings and little else. The whole range of theological "colleges" and "courses" that now exist run on tight budgets while maintaining high standards.

Over the last 30 years or so, the Urban Theology Unit has been a theological resource distinctively and deliberately operating from an inner city plural context. From small beginnings UTU, founded by the Rev Dr John Vincent, has grown and changed into a complex, ecumenical organisation which is a valuable theological
- resource for team ministry, mission and spirituality;
- resource for individuals and organisations campaigning for social justice;
- publisher
- provider of academic courses
- centre for (Methodist) Foundation and Ongoing Ministry Training

UTU's vision is that there is an inseparable relationship between location and learning. While basic learning resources continue to be developed at UTU, the centre of learning is seen to be outside itself in diverse contexts. The wide range of experiences and theologies brought by students provides a rich community of study. Theological education and training is thus enriched by local communities, the peer groups and tutors at UTU. A commitment to those who are poor, and respect for people of different faiths, as reflected in Jesus, represent core UTU values.

In my work with UTU I have found the concept of "a Christian University" helpful. It has been developed at the Jesuit University of Central America (UCA) based in El Salvador. The Christian character of the UCA is discerned to be in its work for the realisation of God's reign of justice and peace and to make real all the values which that entails. Given this vision, the UCA is committed to serving the poor and truth. This is done by studying the situation of the poor, publicly unmasking distortions and announcing truth. Fiction is denounced by announcing facts. The purpose of theological education and training here is to equip the people of God with tools to gather information through digging into the local reality, scripture, sociology, science, tradition, reason, memory and so on, in order that layers of falsehood are removed and good news is unveiled. UCA does this through teaching, research and social outreach. Like the Prophets, the purpose is to declare the truth by unmasking lies and deceit.

"All Universities," says Jon Sobrino of UCA, "have two jobs to do. To take people from ignorance to knowledge, and from falsehood to truth. The former will be termed excellence and funded. The latter may be termed deviant and not funded." For him, a commitment to the poor is essential to the search for truth and the unmasking of lies. For UCA this requires greater academic rigour, not less. Criteria for academic excellence requires, therefore, a commitment to the poor in teaching, research and social outreach.

We are called to be Church now in a world of deep poverty and religious plurality. So, whatever your context, urban, rural, suburban, where you are engaged in Christian discipleship and ministry, lay or ordained, there is a network of theological resource centres near you. How can they assist you to learn in your location? If the UTU style appeals to you, get in touch.

10th May 2001

Disgrace of all Slavery

Hull attracts headlines. Hull East MP, John Prescott, did this by the manner in which he delivered his "man-i-fisto". "From Hull, Hell and Halifax, deliver us Good Lord." A prayer of the days when Hull and Halifax were the last places to have the Gallows, and thus associated with Hell. When John Wesley came to preach in Hull in 1752, he was surprised at "the miserable conditions of the fortifications....ruinous and decayed." Recently, Hull has joined Sheffield as the two cities in Britain reckoned to be the most irreligious and also at the bottom of the scale in terms of economic poverty.

I spent three days in Hull and the surrounding area during Christian Aid Week, while I walked a sponsored 60 miles for the Charity. My route, modified by the Foot and Mouth Crisis, included Hull, Hessle, Cottingham, Beverley, Gilberdyke, Howden, Barmby on the Marsh, Selby, Sheffield, Bishopsthorpe and York. I began at Beverley Minster with Prayer by St John's Tomb.

I was accompanied by Ordinands Beverley Barclay and Sue Sowden, both of whom trained at UTU, Richard Buckley, Anglican Priest and Area Co-ordinator for Christian Aid, Bob Warricker, URC Minister with Sheffield Industrial Mission in South Yorkshire and about 200 others who walked and supported in other ways.

Hull has courageous little Methodist congregations. At Bransholme, one of the largest housing estates in Europe with a population of 32,000, I visited the Methodist Chapel. The building has been destroyed and rebuilt twice in the last 15 years. One member, Daniel, said to me, "They may destroy the building but they won't destroy the people, and its the people who are the Church." The walkers had an early breakfast here, and about thirty members turned out to join us in sharing cereals, large bowls of fruit, and the "Big American Breakfast"!

Hull Docks thrived in the past. They lie dormant now though the Harbour is busy and sees heavy traffic. In the dock area beside the river is Wilberforce House, a Museum now, where William Wilberforce, slavery abolitionist and social reformer, lived. He was born in Hull (1759). We visited the House and were met there by the Mayor and Admiral of the Humber. As we stood by a statue of Wilberforce, I noted the words inscribed below it: "England owes to him the reformation of manners. The World owes to him the abolition of slavery." I asked the Mayor what kind of manners Wilberforce required in England.

Without hesitation she replied, "Respect for all and reverence for all."

William Wilberforce came under the influence of John Wesley's preaching and his "thoughts upon slavery" which saw slavery as a contradiction of God's justice and mercy, and called upon the Captains of the slave trade to "immediately quit the horrid trade." It took twenty years of pressure from Wilberforce, Wesley and others before the Bill for Abolition of the Slave Trade was passed on 24th February 1807. Full emancipation was not achieved until 1834. It took so long because other Members of Parliament had reasons to sustain the slave trade.

The slave trade was indispensable to the British Industrial Revolution which succeeded on the backs of African Slaves. It was well established by the mid-18th century. British ships went from the ports of Bristol, Liverpool and London to Africa, laden with cargoes of cloth, iron, guns and alcohol. These goods were traded for slaves. The ships then sailed, loaded with African children, women and men crammed and chained horizontally in layers below deck in merciless conditions. This killing journey was called "The Middle Passage". In the West Indies the African people were sold as slaves to work on sugar, rice, cotton and tobacco plantations, or as domestic servants. With the money gained, the British traders brought back plantation products to England. This was the Triangular Trade. Millions of Africans died in this Triangle.

Long before Wesley and Wilberforce, the Africans themselves had struggled against slavery. They ran subversive, secret underground routes to bring down the slave owners. Olaudah Equiano gained his freedom and went on to play a strong and eloquent role in the abolition of the slave trade. He visited Hull in 1792. The slave trade was good for Britain. It took 40 years to topple it.

I arrived in Hull wearing my End Debt Bondage lapel chain, my Chain of Office and Jubilee scarf. William Wilberforce said he would "not rest" until the slave trade was abolished. He rests in God, but slavery lives on, and respect and reverence for all is not yet achieved.

A small section in the Wilberforce House Museum is dedicated to awareness of contemporary slavery. There is more slavery today than ever before. Today's slavery includes debt bondage, child labour, servile forms of marriage, forced marriage, cheap migrant labour and cheap house cleaners. Burger Bars are the biggest toy distributors today. What conditions do toy makers work in, what is their "wage", to enable wealthy children to have free toys? What sweaty, cramped low wage conditions of "third world" workers enable people to have cheap CD Players, TVs and so on? How much money do such workers receive for making sporty trainers for which people pay £50, £60, £70 and more? An Amnesty International Report highlighted the appalling slavery of the Dalits in India. Asylum Seekers detained in British Detention Centres are paid £9.50 per week "if they work".

The Christian Aid Walk was a prayer and expression of solidarity with those who are disgraced and exploited in today's slave trades. Prayer is not about telling God what to do, it is not about pushing God until something happens. It is about listening to God and responding with action. We cannot all do prayer walks. But we can all do something.

Slavery is a disgrace and is usually associated with the economy. Jubilee 2000 has demonstrated the power we can all exercise with Government. Vote carefully in the elections. The real economic power, though, lies with multi-national companies and corporations. As consumers we can influence their ethics through careful buying, boycotting and investment. Buy fairly-traded goods. Boycott slave trade goods. Invest ethically. Such action is part of our spiritual and moral obligation, and an act of prayer.

The Christian Aid walk finished by the Pilgrim's Shrine below the Great East Window in York Minster. The windows depict God who is alpha and omega, in whom all creation is held and who watches over all. A reassuring image. I thank all those who supported the walk.

24th May 2001

Fair And Green Isle

"The Flying Barn Door." That's how people of Fair Isle describe the great white tailed eagle. It is now a migrant bird, rarely seen in the British Isles. It hasn't been seen here for five years.

I was honoured with a sighting, just ten yards from where I was, just ten minutes after I'd arrived on Fair Isle in the Shetland Islands. I saw it when it suddenly took flight and soared away showing all its colours. An elegant, majestic bird, with a wing span that gives it its nickname. It flew with gentle slow motion movements. What a privilege to see it.

My host, the Revd. John Best recognised it first, and reached for his camera. I suspect though that the result will show only a spec in the sky.

I had just flown in from Tingwall, Shetland Mainland, in an Islander Plane that was not much bigger than the eagle. The island provides sanctuary for many birds and is a bird watcher's paradise. My main purpose was to meet people, of course, but the birds were determined to be the centre of attraction.

Fair Isle was interpreted for me by different people as the island of sheep, peace, refuge and friendliness. Whatever its correct meaning, all these things and more I found on the Island in good measure. I arrived here having e-mailed a letter to Mr. William Hague on a fair deal for asylum seekers. The letter was crafted on the flight to the Shetland Islands, during which I'd read of Mr. Hague's visit to Dover, and the speech he had delivered there. Wherever we are, Dover, Fair Isle and elsewhere, issues related to racial justice cannot be ignored.

I found the people of Shetland Islands, including the tiny remote Fair Isle, in touch with such matters and responsive to what I had to share.

Most Fair Isle residents have church connections, Methodist or Church of Scotland. The island has two beautiful chapels. Worship is ecumenical, held alternatively in each chapel. The Islanders are searching for a future together. They wondered if "membership" of either denomination makes sense, or whether it is better to form one joint Christian community which expresses its worship in different ways. They wondered whether and for how long they need two centres for worship. These conversations are relevant in so many other contexts, rural and inner-city.

In the Methodist chapel, I sat with John Best, and Stuart Thomson, church steward. They asked for a prayer. We read Psalm 23 and prayed. It was good to be quiet and to listen to the silence, and the song of artic terns and oyster catchers.

We visited many of the residents. There is a great community feeling among them. They are ornithologists, stained-glass experts, meteorologists, jewellers, fishers, sailors, knitters, farmers, crafters, crofters, and every other person seemed to be a Methodist Local Preacher!.

Without planning it this way I concluded my District visits in the Shetland Islands. It was here I came on my first Christian "mission" in April 1974. I was a student at Cliff College at the time, saw an advert in the Church of Scotland magazine 'Life and Work', applied, and joined a Scottish group with Capt. Anderson in Lerwick. I spent a fortnight here, and have always longed to make a return visit. Eric Wright was the Methodist Minister in Lerwick at the time. We've kept in touch since.

When I was in Scalloway I met Eddie. He said he had been "converted" during that "mission" in 1974. He is now a Methodist Local Preacher and Steward and a Pilot. It was Eddie who flew the Islander six-seater plane to Fair Isle. He has worked with the Mission Aviation Fellowship in Kenya, and could converse with me in Swahili a little.

It was great being in Shetland Islands again. The visit was a kind of trip along memory lane. Shetland Islands, too, are among those places and people who are part of my story. I was glad to be there again. The last twenty seven years have brought prosperity and poverty, through the oil industry, with all the ensuing baggage of alcohol and drug abuse to these beautiful islands. I cannot understand why an appointment in Shetland Islands should be seen in negative terms. It may be cold but there are warm and wonderful people here. The air is pure and there is outstanding, natural beauty. I can see why church workers, lay or ordained, once they get here, like to stay here.

On my last morning in Lerwick, I sat on a wall in the harbour and remembered my 1974 visit, and reflected on the journey of my life since then.

I returned home to Sheffield, and saw a different sight in the air. Greenpeace protestors on top of the largest chimney at the city's incinerator plant.

Written large on the chimney were their words: "Toxic Crime". The protest closed down the incinerator. Greenpeace claimed that there had been in excess of 150 breaches of emission levels by the incinerator, making it the worst in Britain.

Sheffield City Council Officials and Parliamentary candidates were critical of the action saying that Greenpeace's allegations were "unfounded".

The general impression among residents in the city is that Sheffield is one of the "greenest cities", and that the incinerator demonstrates this by providing environmentally friendly power to hospitals, homes for the elderly, and many of the city's major buildings including some churches.

However, people who live close to the incinerator speak of their health concerns related to "chemical smoke and smells" emitted from the incinerator. Many people suffer from chest complaints and asthma.

Greenpeace action has certainly made people sit up and take more notice of the incinerator, and raise questions. At what expense to the environment is environmental friendly power being provided?.

Environmental pollution, along with violence of poverty and existence of religious plurality, are challenges that Christian theology and churches will not be able to ignore in the twenty-first century.

So, wherever we are in the British Isles, my time in Shetland Islands and Sheffield raises the question, are we living and working for green and fair isles?

7th June 2001

Methodist Church Music Society – Manchester

All Indian films are musical. I've just finished watching one, and the music includes here the playing of drum beats on clay pots. It took me back to my childhood. An uncle of mine who played drums used to get the children seated around him and got us to bring tunes out of cooking utensils.

My first experience of worship, as a child growing up within the Sikh Community, was one that was dominated by music and song. The Sikh gurus communicated their teaching through songs and poetry that were put to music. This tradition continues to this day. Worship centres on song and music. People are encouraged to write songs, and to offer them in the context of worship.

It has been integral to my thinking therefore that music and songs are aids to the worship of God. The human soul can mingle with the soul of God in singing tuneful songs to God, and in listening to such singing, and in playing or listening to music. One of my regrets is I that I cannot play a musical instrument. I would love to be able to play Tabla. I am not musical but I have a voice and enjoy singing and teaching new songs.

Music and singing is central and integral to Methodist traditions and spirituality. This is certainly one reason why I seek to follow and serve Jesus Christ with Methodists. It is significant that so much of Methodist theology is contained and conveyed in hymns and songs and psalms. Whatever else Methodists have to offer the world, our hymns, songs and psalms are a very special gift. At its best this aspect of Methodist spirituality can be an attraction to others. At its worst and its most boring - it can be a distraction too.

So all that is done to enhance the sung and musical offerings in worship has to be applauded and affirmed. I am glad to do this on behalf of the Methodist Connexion here.

As we seek to enhance our sung and musical offerings in worship we would be all the richer for drawing on world Methodism and are all the poorer if we do not. It is a sad feature of church life and worship that black music for example is generally embraced and enjoyed beyond churches but has yet to find enthusiastic welcome within churches.

People of Asia, Africa, Central and South America, the Pacific – have much to offer the western world in terms of music and song, not least songs in different languages. I want to ask our Methodist Church Music Society to help Methodists in Britain to be enriched by these gifts too. It would be spiritually edifying and fruitful for us all if this were to happen. There is more to music than playing the organ.

- The Western Churches need to recognise in shame that the music and songs of the "third" world or "south" countries were rejected as pagan and were devalued, and banished from church worship. Thankfully, indigenous music is now being restored, affirmed and valued in the south countries. Drums, sticks, sitars, tablas and bajas are to be heard again in church. I am sure that the sounds thrill the heart of God.

- We should rejoice too and share the thrill of God. I want to say to people from "south" countries who are members of churches in Britain - please share all the riches of song and music from your traditions with the Methodist Church in Britain. I want to say to the rest of the Church – please allow this and encourage this contribution.

- It is difficult to state accurately when music began to be used in worship. But of one thing we can be certain – music and song has enhanced the worship of God, and has helped to guard the vitality of the witness of worship against deadening effects of ritual ceremonialism.

- We can be clear also, as seen in Daniel 3, that music with all its wealth and vitality can be used to glorify emperors, state officials and idols too.

- Like Shadrack, Meshak and Abednego – we need a discerning spirit that will keep us from the use of music for idolatrous purposes and help us to use it to assist our worship of God.

- I would love to know more about Jesus and music. Did he and his band of followers often sit into the early hours of the morning and sing and dance and listen to music? All we have to go by is that when he was in need of God's reassurance most, he shared a meal with his friends, and joined them in singing.

4th March 2000

Corrymeela Sunday, Coventry

1977. I was at Hartley Victoria College, engaged in Ministerial Training. The Principal asked if any student would respond to a request from Corrymeela Community in Northern Ireland. They were looking for a volunteer to co-ordinate Community Worship during the months of July and August. I volunteered.

Consequently I paid more attention than usual to news from N Ireland. I listened to experiences of others who had visited N Ireland. The impression I gained was that of bombs, bangs and bullets. One person said to me "you need a coat that is orange on one side and green on the other side. Make sure – as you walk – the green side points towards R. C. areas, and the orange towards Protestant areas. Some of those who had visited N Ireland talked about dodging bullets. They gave the impression of being courageous heroes and heroines who had been to N Ireland. I didn't wish to be a hero. I wished I hadn't volunteered. I was practically a nervous wreck. I didn't know a soul in N Ireland. On top of everything my Asian background and appearance and the colour of my skin would make me stand out. As part of my preparation I read a book called "Divided Ulster," which gave me some background knowledge.

July 1997. I arrived in Larne by ferry. I got off the boat and wondered how to get to Ballycastle and Corrymeela. I felt extremely visible, lonely and vulnerable. From the impression I had gained from others I expected to be caught up in gun fire. Cautiously I approached a port official. "Excuse me. How do I get to Bally castle from here, " I asked. He said, "Go to the bus station. Take a bus to Ballymena: From there take a bus to Ballymoney. Then a bus that will take you to Ballycastle."

"Where's the bus station?" I asked. I must have looked so lone and lost. He looked at me in a concerned way and said, "right, you see the train at the railway station there – go to the driver and ask him to drop you off at the lane that leads to the bus station". So that's what I did. The train set off. One/two minutes later it stopped. I got off. And the train driver pointed me in a direction for the Bus Station – and off I went.

All my stereotypes of N Ireland and its people had been upstaged by the first two people I spoke to in N Ireland. I was still nervous, but much of my fear had been dispelled. The bus to Ballymena, and to Ballymoney and to Ballycastle was a treat. I looked out of the windows and warmed to the beautiful countryside. Some of the street flags, painted curb-stones, wall murals, security vehicles and guarded police stations spoke of political realities.

I came to Ballycastle and phoned Corrymeela. The person I spoke to said, "wait right where you are I'll be with you in 10 minutes and bring you to Corrymeela."

As I sat on a wall by the harbour and Marine Hotel and looked out over the sea I was staggered by the beauty of the area. The majestic Fair Head nods a greeting. Beyond it Scotland – so close, clearly visible.

I was collected by Anna Glass, who is a legendary Corrymeela cook now retired. I was to be wowed by her cooking and Irish recipes and particularly wheaten bread. I have never forgotten, and Anna has never forgotten, that she was the first Corrymeela person I ever met. Her good welcome drove another nail into stereotypes. We became lifelong friends and she has taught me how to bake wheaten bread and much more.

As I caught the first glimpse of Corrymeela House with the Rathlin Island in the background I thought: it is going to be good here. We got out of the car. A woman who was tending a garden around the car park looked up and greeted me. "You're very welcome," she said. Taking her to be the gardener – I chatted with her for a while admiring her work. "What's your name," I asked. "Kathleen" she said.

I was later to discover she was married to the founder of Corrymeela, Ray Davery, and that she is a poet of stature. She has published her poetry since. I was warmly welcomed by a reception team led by Kathleen Bakewell. These first 2 or 3 contacts set the tone.

Everybody I met was welcoming.

I was introduced to the Corrymeela Centre Director, the Revd Harold Good – a Methodist Minister. He introduced me to a Methodist family, from Coleraine, who were there: Donald, Isobel, Steven, Janet and Ruth McDough. Later I organised a placement with Harold at Crumlin Rd Methodist Church. Harold and the McDoughs, and all the others I have named remain good close friends almost 25 years on.

"You're very welcome." These were nearly always the first words of greeting.

And as I got into my role as Worship Co-ordinator, alongside a Servite Priest Brendon O'Brien, I began to feel at home and it did feel good.

The worship was a transforming experience. I was praying with people of catholic and protestant backgrounds, most of whom came from segregated areas in Belfast and Londonderry, people of all ages. So the style of worship was simple, inclusive, participatory, fun. There was no worship centre on site so we used different spaces such as the dining room, lounge, playground, beach, a tent and a building named Coventry House – a name and building that honours a very important relationship. Now the Croi forms the heart of Corrymeela and its worship life.

My approach to worship was changed forever. Simple, inclusive, participatory, and fun remain part of worship. Everybody was so appreciative – I felt I must be doing something right.

I started to help out in other ways. I joined the team of bus drivers. This was significant because it meant I could be with participants in worship a bit more throughout other activities. I met them when I helped to pick them up in Belfast or other places.

I noticed how hardly anyone spoke. People of catholic and protestant backgrounds, who lived apart, were in the same mini-bus. They sat opposite each other. Silence.

At Corrymeela a week-long programme helped them to meet – in worship, at meal times, in outings together to beaches, giant's causeway, they helped each other cross the carrick-a-rede rope bridge, and other bridges; they went on walks together, they shared in Barn Dances, BBQs, concerts; children played together.

They met.
- They came to see each other as human beings and as friends.
- They prayed together.
- They talked and listened to each other and shared each others' hurts and hopes.
- I saw enmity and hatred transformed into empathy and healing.
- I saw people move from identities shared by separatist philosophies, theologies and politics, to seeing that they have shared histories, shared cultures, shared faith journeys, shared space, identities that are inter-twined.
- New relationships were formed.

At the end of the week I noticed that as the people got into the Mini-buses for the returned journeys there were embraces, kisses and tears. People who wouldn't sit with each other seemed now to be inseparable. They had moved from separatism to acknowledgment that people locked in separate worlds can move toward embracing each other. The return journey to their homes was certainly not a silent one. It was full of talk, laughter and songs.

Quite often I had to stay overnight in Belfast, and usually one of the families would volunteer to give me a bed. I got to stay in most parts of Belfast. I learned much from those overnight stops. It became clear to me that though a week at Corrymeela was significant for families, the impact of a 300 year history would not be completely altered in seven days.

Yet I am sure that in 30 years Corrymeela Community and its supporters have made a huge contribution towards the removal of stereotypes, misrepresentations and demonisation of others, the process of peace, justice, reconciliation, healing and unity we are in now.

In addition to all else Corrymeela does, the summer programmes work with family groups, and other groups have been the core for me.

In the early days I returned during all my summer holidays from college to share in this work, for the whole of July and August. Obviously I had more energy when I was in my early 20s. Now I spend a week as a volunteer at Corrymeela and I am exhausted.

My first ministry appointment was to churches in multi-faith Wolverhampton, where for 3 years I was also co-ordinator of the Wolverhampton inter-faith group. The lessons I learned in Ireland were extremely useful. It had become clear to me that in a plural, multi-faith society:

1)   The potential for separatist development exists with all the ensuing dangers of scapegoating the "others" for all the social ills, and demonisation, misrepresention and stereotyping of "others".

2)   The need in such contexts to help people from different faiths and ideologies to meet, to build trust, and to form relationships of mutual respect.

3)   The recognition in a plural society that all the parties must be involved in dialogue.

In Wolverhampton I used the skills I learned at Corrymeela and in N Ireland. I remain convinced now, as before, that people of different faiths and ideologies and skin colours and politics – in cities like Coventry, Belfast, Birmingham and Wolverhampton need to meet. Somebody, somewhere needs to take the initiative to facilitate such meetings.

The lessons of Corrymeela have to be applied everywhere.

Over the last 30 years I have heard Corrymeela echo the following words of a discussion document entitled *Sectarianism*, submitted in 1993 to the Irish inter-church meeting:

People need to "find a way of living together in difference without wanting to dominate, destroy or separate" (p 40) - And to ask these questions:

"How can we live together without denying differences or the truth as we see it? And can we go beyond such peaceful co-existence into some fuller, more positive relationship? (p 47)

The report begins to see the answer emerging in the words of the Gospel: "treat others as you would like them to treat you". (p 47)

The inter-church report on violence in Ireland had said in 1976 that an end to sectarianism must be found in Ireland. But sectarianism is not just a phenomenon of Ireland. It is an international reality, not least here in Britain. Sectarianism in Britain takes the form of racial discrimination and attacks on Mosques, Synagogues, Gurdwaras, Mandirs, and so on; and it takes the form of racial attacks symbolised for the world in the story of Stephen Lawrence.

Difference is an important theme in theology and world politics in the contemporary world, especially in the cities. There are people around the world who are saying to others: "you are different from me – we cannot live with you - you live somewhere else." An attitude that gives rise to contemporary forms of apartheid in ethnic cleansing and sectarianism. Racism is a form sectarianism.

Today we honour Corrymeela, and all those who point us to the path we need to take if we are not to destroy each other.

At around the season of Lent we honour these people, martyrs of the contemporary world: MK Gandhi, D Bonhoeffer, M L King, Oscar Romero ...

and we think of those over 3000 lives lost in Ireland. How are we to remain who we are, to see truth as we do, to remain rooted to our own history, heritage, humanity, culture – and still reach out to others in respect?

What do we need to do as Christians, as churches, - what are the ways we must help develop if we are to help people – including ourselves – to live as different people without wanting to dominate, destroy or separate?

I keep returning to N Ireland and to Corrymeela for help and inspiration. I keep returning because Ireland is so beautiful, its people so welcoming and hospitable, yet so demonised, misrepresented and maligned.

For many years I have taken groups with me
- an interfaith group from Wolverhampton
- ecumenical groups from Sheffield
- I am taking 40 in Easter week this year, flying from Sheffield Airport to Belfast city harbour airport.

One of my favourite spots on earth is Ballintoy harbour. It's a gorgeous spot to sit quietly and to watch the waves beating on the rocks, and to watch gannets diving for their food, and to watch the fishermen go out and come in and sometimes to buy a mackerel or two from them.

I keep returning to Ireland because I feel people are dealing with issues which matter to me, issues around the theme of identity, history, culture, language, and music. I return now also because my family demands visits to Corrymeela. My children enjoy Corrymeela, and like to help there. They are budding future volunteers.

The church where I am based likes to visit Corrymeela. 30 of them will accompany me at Easter, as will student ministers training at the Urban Theology Unit. I have, of course, strong links with the Methodist church in Ireland and may have to chair the Irish Methodist Conference in June 2001. I have organised many Corrymeela events in Britain, including Corrymeela Sunday celebrations in Wolverhampton and Sheffield.

I find great theological insights and inspiration in Ireland, not least in the work and publications of the Faith and Politics Group of the Inter-Church meeting.

Latterly I have become very interested in the Asian population of Ireland, 15,000 or so. This section of the population has experienced the brunt of sectarianism too, and in some ways ceasefires have not meant an end to attacks on those who are different because of the colour of skin. A workable peace in Ireland must include the hurts and hopes of all people of all faiths.

- Britain has much to learn from the integrated education developments in Ireland. In Britain there is an alarming trend towards separation in education.
- Britain has much to learn from Ireland about policing and prisoners in areas of terrorism.

It would be easy to give in to a sense of hopelessness in the face of complex and apparently remote issues. It would be easy to dismiss them as "the Irish problem". It is not the Irish problem. There are British responsibilities. People in England, Scotland, Wales and Ireland have a part to play in seeking a just and peaceful future for Britain and Ireland. The on-off peace process needs to be sustained and strengthened. We can all do something. We can pray that God will show all involved the pathways to justice and peace. We can give more attention to trying to listen to people of Ireland and understanding the issues involved - not least by visiting Ireland. At least our prayers will be more informed as a result.

Let me conclude with one particular memory. I remember standing outside Corrymeela house on one visit, trying to locate a comet in a sky full of stars. In a way, that image, a comet in a sky full of stars, symbolises Corrymeela for me. Many organisations and individuals in Ireland, including the Corrymeela community, are sharing the uneasy peace process flickering and fragile as a flame of a candle. The commitment to remembering, truth telling, penitence, forgiveness, justice, change, reconciliation, healing and unity is strong. I believe we can all do something through genuine partnership which is based on mutuality, trust and respect. A partnership can mean having to stop, and go over to the other side to offer support, but also speaks about a humility which has the capacity to receive.

People in Ireland have a long history of learning to live with diversity. People throughout Europe and the world can learn from this – not least we in cities like Sheffield, Wolverhampton, Birmingham and Coventry.

12th March 2000